| Date Due | | | |
|---|---|---|---|
| Nov 29'62 | Mar 17 | | |
| Feb 20'63 | | | |

Jι

[

# SHAKESPEARE
## AS COLLABORATOR

# Shakespeare
## as Collaborator

### KENNETH MUIR

*King Alfred Professor of English Literature
in the University of Liverpool*

NEW YORK
BARNES & NOBLE INC

TO THE MEMORY
OF TWO ELIZABETHAN SCHOLARS
UNA ELLIS-FERMOR
ARNOLD DAVENPORT

# Contents

# Preface

This book, though it incorporates revised versions of five articles written during the past ten years, is based partly on four lectures delivered at Stratford-upon-Avon under the auspices of the University of Birmingham. I am indebted to Professor Terence Spencer, the Director of the Summer School in 1959, and also to Dr Louis B. Wright for enabling me to spend three happy and profitable months at the Folger Shakespeare Library. I have to thank Miss M. Barber for permission to quote from marginalia by the late Professor Una Ellis-Fermor.

The scope of the book is deliberately restricted. I have not attempted to deal with all the plays which publishers and critics have ascribed to Shakespeare, but only with those plays which, though excluded from the First Folio, show unmistakable traces of his hand, and with the lost play, *Cardenio*.

The classical demonstration of the presence of Shakespeare's hand in an apocryphal play is that of the late R. W. Chambers in *Man's Unconquerable Mind*. Few readers of that brilliant essay are left in any doubt that Shakespeare contributed at least one scene to *Sir Thomas More*. I have relied largely on similar methods in my attempt to prove that Shakespeare was partly responsible for *Edward III* and *The Two Noble Kinsmen*; but I have learnt also from R. B. Heilman's *This Great Stage* and *Magic in the Web*,

# Preface

from F. C. Kolbe's *Shakespeare's Way*, from R. A. Foakes' important essay in *Shakespeare Survey 5* and from G. Wilson Knight's numerous books on Shakespeare. Under the term 'imagery' I include, in accordance with much modern practice, not merely metaphors and similes but the iteration of significant words and symbols. There is no gold imagery, in the narrow sense, in *Timon of Athens*, but gold is clearly used as a significant symbol. There is hardly any Time imagery in *Troilus and Cressida*, but the iteration of time is as important as the cooking imagery analysed by Caroline Spurgeon.

I have also made use of image-clusters as a means of detecting Shakespeare's hand. The first critic to point out an image-cluster was Walter Whiter, who, a century and a half ago, pointed out the association in Shakespeare's mind of flatterers, dogs, and melting sweets. Although, of course, dogs and flattery are associated in other writers, the triple association in its obsessive form appears to be peculiar to Shakespeare. A few more clusters were pointed out by Caroline Spurgeon, and Edward A. Armstrong analysed a number of others in *Shakespeare's Imagination*. Although clusters have been discovered in the work of other Elizabethan poets, and although some of the associations pointed out by Mr Armstrong are not unexpected, the presence of the same clusters in doubtful plays and the absence of these clusters in the work of rival claimants, seems to me to go far to establish the presence of Shakespeare's hand. An imaginary example will make this point clear. A modern poet, old enough to remember the sinking of the *Titanic*, might years later associate Titan, ice, shipwreck and death. He might even associate the hymn 'Abide with me' with the same words. Such associations

# Preface

might be found in the work of several poets born between 1900 and 1907. But suppose that one of these poets had lost his Uncle David in the same disaster, Uncle David and Goliath might be added to the cluster; and a critic a century hence might well be puzzled to observe that nearly every time this poet mentioned *ice*, he would, within the next few lines, refer to the story of David and Goliath. If the critic were to come across an anonymous poem with the same peculiarity he would surely be justified in claiming it for the same poet:

> He felt the clutch of ice upon his heart,
> But knew that with Faith's sling he could bring down
> The giant Fear.

The presence of such a private association, in spite of the feebleness of the lines, would authenticate his work as certainly as the signature Vincent on a Van Gogh painting. Some, but not all, of the clusters found in Shakespeare's works appear to be equally significant, since an imitator is quite unlikely to have had precisely the same associations.

I should add that I am grateful for the advice of Dr G. K. Hunter and Mr Ernest Schanzer, both of whom read the book in manuscript, and to the criticism of Professor Harold Jenkins. Acknowledgements are due to the editors of *Shakespeare Survey*, *English Studies* and *Etudes Anglaises* for permission to reprint, though with substantial modifications, Chapters II and VI, Chapter IV, and Chapter VIII respectively.

KENNETH MUIR

*Liverpool*                                    *August* 1959

# I

# Introduction

The First Folio, published in 1623, contained thirty-six plays of Shakespeare. As the editors, Hemminge and Condell, were members of Shakespeare's own company, there is no reason to doubt that they included all the plays they believed to be his, at least those of which they could obtain adequate texts. Some critics, even today, believe that Shakespeare was not wholly responsible for *Henry VI*, *Titus Andronicus*, and *Henry VIII*; but no responsible critic doubts that Shakespeare was at least part author of all the plays contained in the Folio. Hemminge and Condell's inclusions were sound. But there is some evidence that for one reason or another they did not include all the plays in which Shakespeare had a hand. Meres mentions a *Love's Labours Won*, and some new evidence for the existence of a play of that title has recently been discovered by Professor Baldwin. It has not come down to us under that title, but it may be an alternative title of *All's Well that Ends Well*, or (if we are to believe Professor Leslie Hotson) of *Troilus and Cressida*. A play was performed at Court by Shakespeare's company in 1613, apparently entitled *Cardenio*, and based on an episode in *Don Quixote*. It was advertised by the publisher of Milton's minor poems as being by Shakespeare and Fletcher. Hemminge and Condell did not include this in the Folio. *Pericles* was published as Shakespeare's in his lifetime, and it contains scenes which no one denies are his; but it may have been excluded from the Folio because the editors were unable to obtain a better text than the deplorable one contained in the bad quarto of 1609. Then there was *The Two Noble Kinsmen*, published in 1634, and ascribed by the publisher to Shakespeare and Fletcher. Although some modern critics assume that Hemminge and Condell were right to exclude it, and that Fletcher's collaborator was Massinger rather than Shakespeare, most critics would now agree that Shakespeare had a hand in it. There is reason to believe that Shakespeare contributed at least one scene to the banned play of *Sir Thomas More*, and it has been forcibly argued that he wrote part of *Edward III*. There is no real evidence that he wrote any of the other plays which have been ascribed to him by unscrupulous and ignorant publishers and by eccentric critics.

More than a score of plays have been ascribed on their title-pages to Shakespeare or to W. S. – initials which could signify Wentworth Smith, William Smith, or William Sly as well as Shakespeare. Some of these plays – *Thomas Lord Cromwell*, *The London Prodigal*, and *A Yorkshire Tragedy* – were performed by Shakespeare's company, and this fact may have influenced the mistaken attribution. Others (*Edward II*, *The Spanish Tragedy*, *The Arraignment of Paris*, for example) are known to be by other dramatists. Six of these apocryphal plays were included in the Third Folio (1664) for no better reason than that they had already been ascribed to Shakespeare and were not definitely known to be by another dramatist; but neither

2

# Introduction

*The Two Noble Kinsmen* nor *Edward III* was published in this Folio. The favoured six were *Locrine* (1595), *I Sir John Oldcastle* (1600), *Thomas Lord Cromwell* (1602), *The London Prodigal* (1605), *The Puritan* (1607), and *A Yorkshire Tragedy* (1608). Four of these plays are admirably discussed in Baldwin Maxwell's *Studies in the Shakespeare Apocrypha*, and he comes to the conclusion (with which all must concur) that Shakespeare had no hand in any of them.[1] Max Moltke, who chose six plays for the Tauchnitz edition in 1869 (including the four discussed by Maxwell), declared that he had selected 'those six pieces which, according to my firm conviction, bear the most unmistakable traces of Shakespeare's authorship'; but in spite of his firm conviction a reasoned case can be made out for only one of the six, *Edward III*.

The external evidence for Shakespeare's authorship of plays not included in the First Folio is therefore quite unsubstantial. We are driven to rely on internal evidence, which, from the nature of things, is somewhat subjective. Some critics, for example, have professed to find Shakespeare's hand in the best of the apocryphal plays, *Arden of Feversham*; but it does not resemble in style or theme any of Shakespeare's acknowledged plays. Although, theoretically, he might have varied his style to suit the theme, it is difficult to believe that he could have written a play which has no points of contact with his others. *The Comedy of Errors*, *Hamlet*, and *Cymbeline* are three plays totally different from each other in theme, style, and treatment; and yet it could be shown that they were by

[1] See K. Muir, *T.L.S.* (1944), p. 391, for a discussion of the relationship between *Locrine* and *Selimus*.

3

the same author even if they had not all been included in the First Folio.

In the following chapters we shall consider what internal evidence has been adduced for the Shakespearian authorship of apocryphal plays. The evidence includes resemblances in versification, in vocabulary, in treatment of similar themes, in imagery, and the use of the same image clusters. Versification tests are mainly negative: they can be used to show that one or other known dramatist is unlikely to have written the scene under discussion, or to show that the scene has the same metrical characteristics as scenes written by Shakespeare at one period of his career. Vocabulary tests have been used to show that an apocryphal scene contains unusual words to be found also in Shakespeare's acknowledged works; and, more fruitfully, to show that the incidence of words not before used by Shakespeare and of coinages corresponds to the incidence in his acknowledged plays. Imagistic tests may be used to prove that the proportion of images drawn from different fields corresponds to the proportion in Shakespeare's plays or to demonstrate the presence of similar iterative imagery. Perhaps the strongest evidence for the Shakespearian authorship of an apocryphal scene is the presence of an image-cluster to be found in Shakespeare's works but not yet discovered in the works of other dramatists. (See p. x above.)

The Shakespearian authorship of part of *Sir Thomas More* is now accepted by all competent critics, and there is nothing that need be added to the powerful arguments of Professor J. Dover Wilson, Caroline Spurgeon, Sir Edward Maunde Thompson, and R. W. Chambers, supported by several later critics.[1] The play was written by several authors – Chettle, Heywood, and Dekker – and apparently revised by Shakespeare; but it failed to comply with the demands of Tilney, the censor, and it was not performed until the present century. Tilney demanded the omission of the scenes dealing with the insurrection; and though Shakespeare's revision exhibits a very tame and amenable mob, and More is given eloquent and persuasive speeches in favour of submission, Tilney was apparently adamant. The mob in *Coriolanus* is much more dangerous; but presumably the question of aliens was a more inflammable topic in London than the Midlands insurrection, which is thought to be reflected in the later play.

*Sir Thomas More* is a special case, because one scene in the manuscript is in a handwriting several experts have believed to be Shakespeare's; and if the handwriting is Shakespeare's he must have been the author of the scene, since it is palpably a first draft. Sir Edward Maunde Thompson pointed out several peculiarities common to Shakespeare's signatures, and the handwriting of this scene – the so-called spurred *a*; an unusual *k*; the formation of a *p*; the use of an Italian form for the long S; and the use of a downstroke partially covered by an upstroke and thus forming 'an elongated needle-eye'. Against this it has been argued that Chapman used both the spurred *a*

[1] *Shakespeare's Hand in the Play* of 'Sir Thomas More' (1923); R. W. Chambers, *Man's Unconquerable Mind*; Caroline Spurgeon, *R.E.S.* (1930), pp. 257–70; J. M. Nosworthy *R.E.S.* (1955), pp. 12 ff.; R. C. Bald, *Shakespeare Survey 2*, pp. 44 ff. I. A. Shapiro, *Shakespeare Survey 8*, pp. 100–5, argues that *Sir Thomas More* must have been written not later than 1591 and that Shakespeare's scene was added in 1593.

and the elongated needle-eye, though Chapman cannot have written the scene;[1] but Sir Walter Greg was probably right in saying that the 'palaeographic case for the hands of Shakespeare and D (in *Sir Thomas More*) being the same is stronger than can be made out for their being different'.

The palaeographic evidence, strong as it is, is supported by the evidence of spellings. Dover Wilson showed that some of the spellings in the three pages of *Sir Thomas More* can be paralleled in some odd spellings which have survived in the good quartos of Shakespeare's plays; and that some of the misprints in the quartos can be explained on the assumption that the compositor was faced with a handwriting similar to that of Hand D.

But even if there were no manuscript of *Sir Thomas More* there would be good reason for believing that Shakespeare was the author of this addition. R. W. Chambers and Caroline Spurgeon have shown by an examination of the imagery, the style, the sequences of thought, and the characterization in the scene that Shakespeare must have written it. The fickle mob, illogical, ignorant, and violent as it is, is depicted not without humorous touches, and not without some sympathy, and it is easily shamed into repentance. Perhaps the best example of humour and of the illogicality of the mob is in the passage about parsnips:

> *Lincoln.* They bring in strange roots, which is merely to the undoing of your prentices, for what's a sorry parsnip to a good heart?

[1] The style is totally unlike that of Chapman's early plays.

# Introduction

*William.* Trash, trash: they breed sore eyes and 'tis enough
to infect the city with the palsy.

*Lincoln.* Nay, it has infected it with the palsy, for these
bastards of dung – as you know they grow in dung – have
infected us, and it is our infection will make the city shake
– which partly comes through the eating of parsnips.

*Clown.* True, and pumpions together.

Lincoln apparently confuses *infection* and *insurrection*, and
suggests that there is some connexion between the
shaking of the city by their riot and the trembling of a
fit of the palsy. The Cade scenes in *Henry VI* and the mob
scenes in *Julius Caesar* and *Coriolanus* seem to have been
written by the same hand.

In Ulysses' speech on order in *Troilus and Cressida*, in
one of Albany's speeches in *King Lear*, and in *Coriolanus*
it is suggested that the breakdown of order in the State
may lead to cannibalism. As Albany puts it:

> Humanity must perforce prey on itself
> Like monsters of the deep.

The association of disorder and cannibalism is, as far as
we know, peculiar to Shakespeare; but in one of More's
speeches in which he is attacking the mob for wishing to
banish the aliens he says:

> Grant them removed, and grant that this your noise
> Have chid down all the majesty of England:
> Imagine that you see the wretched strangers
> Their babies at their backs, and their poor luggage
> Plodding to th' ports and coasts for transportation,
> And that you sit as kings in your desires,
> Authority quite silenced by your brawl,
> And you in ruff of your opinions clothed,

## Shakespeare as Collaborator

What had you got? I'll tell you: you had taught
How insolence and strong hand should prevail,
How order should be quelled, and by this pattern
Not one of you should live an aged man –
For other ruffians as their fancies wrought,
With self same hand, self reasons and self right
Would shark on you, and men like ravenous fishes
Would feed on one another.

Apart from the image of the ravenous fishes, the whole rhythm and movement of the speech is palpably Shakespearian, and phrase after phrase reminds us of the master.

The Shakespearian authorship of this scene is now generally accepted; and one other speech of More's, though not in Shakespeare's handwriting, appears to have the genuine Shakespearian ring, and it stands out clearly from the rest of the scene in which it appears.

It is in heaven that I am thus and thus,
And that which we profanely term our fortunes
Is the provision of the power above,
Fitted and shaped just to that strength of nature
Which we were born withal. Good God, good God,
That I, from such an humble bench of birth,
Should step as 'twere up to my country's head,
And give the law out there: I, in my father's life,
To take prerogative and tithe of knees
From elder kinsmen, and him bind by my place
To give the smooth and dexter way to me,
That owe it him by nature. Sure, these things,
Not physicked by respect, might turn our blood
To much corruption. But More, the more thou hast,
Either of honour, office, wealth and calling,

8

Which might accite thee to embrace and hug them,
The more do thou in serpents' natures think them,
Fear their gay skins with thought of their sharp state,
And let this be thy maxim: to be great
Is, when the thread of hazard is once spun,
A bottom great wound up, greatly undone.

As Shakespeare took no part in planning *Sir Thomas More*, any discussion of the dramatic merits of the play as a whole lies outside the scope of this book. The three plays with which we are concerned in the chapters which follow will be considered both from the point of view of authorship and from the point of view of dramatic value.

## II

# Shakespeare's Hand in *Edward III*

Since 1760, when Capell claimed that *Edward III* was written by Shakespeare, its authorship has been discussed by numerous critics. In the nineteenth century Tennyson, Ward, and Fleay believed that the Countess scenes were Shakespearian, while Swinburne, Saintsbury, Symonds, and Moore Smith denied their authenticity. In the present century Tucker Brooke, while admitting that these scenes were much more Shakespearian at first sight than the rest of the play, came to the conclusion that they were by the same author as the remaining scenes, and that this author was George Peele.[1] F. W. Moorman argued that Shakespeare revised the play between 1590 and 1596, and that he completely rewrote the Countess scenes.[2] R. M. Smith showed that Froissart provided the main source of the play, and that the Countess episode was derived from this source as well as from Painter's *Palace of Pleasure*.[3] Smith, however, went beyond the evidence when he concluded that the whole play must have been written 'at one time by one playwright', and that this playwright could not have been Shakespeare. At about the same time Platt argued that as 'lilies that

[1] *Shakespeare Apocrypha*, xx–xxiii.    [2] C.H.E.L. V. 246.
[3] J.E.G.P. X (1911), 90–104.

fester smell far worse than weeds' and 'scarlet ornaments' were both more appropriate to their contexts in the *Sonnets* than to those in the play, the unknown author must have seen some of the sonnets in manuscript.[1] Sir Edmund Chambers cautiously supported the view that Shakespeare wrote not only the Countess scenes, but also IV. iv.[2] Finally, Alfred Hart, by means of vocabulary tests, came to the conclusion that the whole play must be either by Shakespeare or by some author unknown – not by Peele, Greene, or Marlowe.[3]

Such is the present state of the controversy in which Swinburne has argued most persuasively against the attribution of the play to Shakespeare,[4] and Hart has presented the most 'scientific' case for his authorship. Swinburne relied entirely on aesthetic arguments. He thought the author was 'a devout student and humble follower' of Marlowe; that the faults of the play were due, not to haste or carelessness, but to 'lifelong and ir-remediable impotence' of a 'conscientious and studious workman of technically insufficient culture and of naturally limited means'; that although there are stray lines reminiscent of Shakespeare, 'the structure, the com-position, is feeble, incongruous, inadequate and effete'; and that resemblances to Shakespeare are due to the fact that in his early plays 'the style of Shakespeare was not for the most part distinctively his own'. Swinburne then devoted some twenty pages to an analysis of the Countess

[1] M.L.R. vi (1911), 511–13.
[2] *William Shakespeare* (1930), I. 515.
[3] *Shakespeare and the Homilies* (1934), 219–41.
[4] *A Study of Shakespeare* (1879; ed. 1918), 231–75.

scenes. He thought that the speech containing the Shakespearian phrase, 'scarlet ornaments' (II. i. 1–24), is 'but just better than what is utter intolerable'; that Warwick's lines (II. i. 443–7) 'vaguely remind the reader of something better read elsewhere'; and that the passage containing the other quotation from the *Sonnets* (II. i. 447 ff.) appears more like

> a theft from Shakespeare's private store of undramatic poetry than a misapplication by its own author to dramatic purposes of a line too apt and exquisite to endure without injury the transference from its original setting.

Swinburne's intimate knowledge of Elizabethan drama gives more weight to his opinion than Tennyson's; but, as so frequently with his criticism, this essay appears to be coloured by personal animosity.[1]

On the other side of the controversy, some of Hart's vocabulary tests appear to be inconclusive.[2] His most

[1] Swinburne illustrates the incompetence of the author by the phrase 'helly spout of blood' (a misprint for 'Hellespont of blood'). Some of his arguments fall to the ground if it is accepted that *Measure for Measure* was written after *Edward III* – for the author could not have imitated a yet unwritten play of Shakespeare's. The real problem is whether Shakespeare was echoing his own work or that of another dramatist.

[2] The following tests are inconclusive: (*a*) The average number of words used in some of Shakespeare's Histories is not very different from the number used in *Edward III*, nor very different from the average number used in some of Marlowe's plays. (*b*) The vocabulary common to *Edward III* and some of Shakespeare's Histories is not very different in proportion to the vocabulary common to *Edward III* and some of Marlowe's plays. (*c*) Nor is there any significant difference in the use of certain prefixes and suffixes in *Edward III*, in some of Shakespeare's Histories, and in some of Marlowe's plays.

significant one deals with the use of Compound Participial Adjectives, by which he shows that Shakespeare was twice as fond as Marlowe of the different kinds of adjectival compounds, and three times as fond of them as Greene or Peele. As the figures for *Edward III* approximate to those of Shakespeare, it is reasonable to assume, at least, that the play was not written by one of these University Wits. Another of Hart's tests – which he does not himself apply to *Edward III* – is that of the occurrence of words not used before in Shakespeare's plays. If one divides the play into two parts – (A) the possibly Shakespearian scenes, I. ii. 90 ff., II, IV. iv, (B) the rest of the play – one finds that the incidence of new words in A is twice as frequent as in B. This would seem to suggest that the play was not written by a single author.

On the other hand, Miss Mary Bell has recently argued [1] that a study of the compounds used in *Edward III* provides evidence of single authorship

for the proportion in each part of the play conforms reasonably to the number of lines; and, in addition, there are inspired and original formations in each section. Thus in the Countess scenes we find 'light borne', 'under garnished', 'summer leaping', 'sole reigning', 'bed-blotting', 'honey gathering' and 'poison sucking'; and in part B 'ever bibbing', 'Bayard-like' (which may be linked with 'haggard-like' 'lion-like' and a frequent use of 'warlike') 'high-swollen', 'iron-harted', 'sweet-flowering', 'stiff-grown', 'nimble-jointed', 'swift-starting' and 'just-dooming', to mention only a few.

[1] In an unpublished thesis, Liverpool (1959), p. 112.

Yet, as Miss Bell recognizes, it must be noticed that while all the '-like' compounds appear in part B, all the six 'thrice-' formations are in part A.

Miss Bell further shows that a comparison of *Henry VI* and *Edward III* reveals a close relationship between the vocabulary of the four plays. A large number of words used by Shakespeare only once, in *Henry VI*, are to be found also in *Edward III*. This evidence is ambiguous, since some critics still believe that *Henry VI* is not wholly Shakespearian.

A study of the imagery of *Edward III* reveals some interesting results.[1] First, there are about twice as many images, in proportion to the number of lines, in the scenes ascribed to Shakespeare as in the other scenes – one image every 3·8 lines compared with one every 7 lines. This may, perhaps, be due to the difference of subject-matter. Secondly, there appears to be iterative imagery in the play, which will be analysed below. Thirdly, there are a number of images which resemble those in Shakespeare's plays, and some of them are linked together by quibbles, as Shakespeare's often are.[2]

The iterative imagery is particularly apparent in the scenes which have been ascribed to Shakespeare (A), though there are traces of it in the other scenes (B). In the following table of selected groups of images it should be remembered that the number of lines in the B scenes is about twice as many as those in the A scenes:

[1] Caroline Spurgeon left no notes on the play.
[2] Cf. Kenneth Muir, 'The Uncomic Pun' (*Cambridge Journal*, May 1950) and M. M. Mahood, *Shakespeare's Word Play* (1957).

| Field | Total | A | B |
|---|---|---|---|
| Clothes, Masking, Disguise | 28 | 17 | 11 |
| Metals, buying and selling | 36 | 30 | 6 |
| Sun, Moon, and Stars | 23 | 22 | 1 |
| War | 23 | 14 | 9 |
| Poison | 10 | 7 | 3 |
| Crime, Punishment, Law | 16 | 14 | 2 |

These seem to be the most significant groups of images, for the nature images (83), frequent in most poets, and those drawn from books (10) have no particular, or interpretable, dramatic function. The first of the groups tabulated brings out the contrast between appearance and reality, and between true beauty and false:

These ragged walles no testimonie are,
What is within . . .
(I. ii. 157)

And trueth hath puld the visard from his face . . .
(I. i. 77)

Apparaled sin in vertuous sentences . . .
(II. i. 410)

Decke an Ape
In tissue, and the beautie of the robe
Adds but the greater scorne vnto the beast.
(II. i. 444)

Away, loose silkes of wauering vanitie . . .
(II. ii. 94)

15

my passion,
Which he shall shadow with a vaile of lawne . . .
(II. i. 55)

And with the strumpets artifitiall line
To painte thy vitious and deformed cause,
Bee well assured, the counterfeit will fade,
And in the end thy fowle defects be seene . . .
(III. iii. 81)

Clothing and disguise images are used for much the same purpose in *Much Ado about Nothing* – and, indeed, in much Elizabethan literature.

The images taken from the precious metals and treasure symbolize the value of love and also the counterfeit nature of adultery, thus linking up with the previous group:

She is all the Treasure of our land . . .
(II. i. 45)

And be enriched by thy soueraignes loue . . .
(II. i. 75)

Whie dost thou tip mens tongues with golden words
And peise their deedes with weight of heauie leade . . .
(II. i. 303)

But soft, here comes the treasurer of my spirit . . .
(II. i. 184)

Of her, whose ransackt treasurie hath taskt
The vaine indeour of so many pens . . .
(II. ii. 196)

He that doth clip or counterfeit your stamp
Shall die, my Lord; and will your sacred selfe
Comit high treason against the King of heauen.

To stamp his Image in forbidden mettel,
Forgetting your alleageance and your othe?
(II. i. 255)

When thou conuertest from honors golden name . . .
(II. i. 456)

like a Country swaine,
Whose habit rude and manners blunt and playne
Presageth nought, yet inly beautified
With bounties, riches and faire hidden pride.
For where the golden Ore doth buried lie,
The ground, vndeckt with natures tapestrie
Seemes barrayne . . .
(I. ii. 145)

The images from the sun, moon, and stars, as in Elizabethan sonnet sequences, including Shakespeare's, are
used to symbolize love and beauty:

Now, in the Sunne alone it doth not lye,
With light to take light from a mortall eye . . .
(I. ii. 131)

For here two day stars that myne eies would see
More then the Sunne steales myne owne light from mee.
(I. ii. 133)

thy presence, like the Aprill sunne . . .
(I. ii. 141)

What is she, when the sunne lifts vp his head,
But like a fading taper, dym and dead?
(II. i. 145)

And, being vnmaskt, outshine the golden Sun . . .
(II. i. 148)

Say shee hath thrice more splendour then the sun,
That her perfections emulats the sunne,
That she breeds sweets as plenteous as the sunne,
That she doth thaw cold winter like the sunne,
That she doth cheare fresh sommer like the sunne,
That shee doth dazle gazers like the sunne;
And, in this application to the sunne,
Bid her be free and generall as the sunne,
Who smiles vpon the basest weed that growes
As louinglie as on the fragrant rose.

(II. i. 156)

like an humble shaddow
Yt hauntes the sunshine of my summers life . . .

(II. i. 232)

Alas, she winnes the sunne of me,
For that is she her selfe.

(II. ii. 69)

But loue hath eyes as iudgement to his steps,
Till too much loued glory dazzles them.

(II. ii. 72)

The images from war, natural to the battle scenes, symbolize in the love scenes the attack on the Countess's chastity:

Vnnaturall beseege!

(II. i. 412)

A lingring English seege of peeuish loue . . .

(II. i. 23)

What bewtie els could triumph ouer me . . .

(II. i. 97)

18

The quarrell that I haue requires no armes
But these of myne . . .
(II. ii. 63)

My eyes shall be my arrowes, and my sighes
Shall serue me as the vantage of the winde,
To wherle away my sweetest artyllerie.
(II. ii. 66)

My follies seege against a faithfull louer . . .
(II. ii. 209)

Giue me an Armor of eternall steele!
I go to conquer kings; and shall I not then
Subdue my selfe?
(II. ii. 98)

thy Soule is all too proud
To yeeld her Citie for one little breach.
(IV. ix. 44)

The images from poison, and from crime and punishment, emphasize the corruption of unlawful passion:

Which shoots infected poyson in my heart . . .
(I. ii. 129)

a poison-sucking enuious spider
To turne the iuce I take to deadlie venom . . .
(II. i. 284)

What can one drop of poyson harme the Sea,
Whose hugie vastures can digest the ill
And make it loose his operation?
(II. i. 401)

And giue the bitter potion of reproch
A sugred, sweet and most delitious tast . . .
(II. i. 405)

19

That poyson shewes worst in a golden cup . . .
(II. i. 449)

O periurde beautie, more corrupted Iudge!
When to the great Starre-chamber ore our heads
The vniuersall Sessions cals to count
This packing euill, we both shall tremble for it.
(II. ii. 164)

One characteristic of Shakespeare's use of imagery is the presence of what Edward A. Armstrong calls image-clusters, groups of unconsciously associated words which reappear in play after play. He has argued that these clusters can be used as a test of authorship,[1] even though traces of them have been found in Marlowe. One of the clusters he analyses, that of the Eagle and the Drone, appears in *Edward III*, where in the first scene (94 ff.) we have *drone, eagle, creeping, stealth, nightingale, voluntary* (music), and *grudging* (mood). In *2 Henry VI* (IV. i. 102 ff.) we find *drone, eagle, crept, suck*, and *rob*. (In the *Edward III* context there is mention of a storm, and in *Henry VI* of thunder.) In *Henry V* (I. ii. 170 ff.) we get *drone, eagle, sneaking, sucks, thieves, weasel, cat, music*, and *surly*. As we should expect from a study of such clusters, the *Edward III* example is larger than that in *Henry VI*, which was written earlier, and smaller than that in the later play, *Henry V*. But for several reasons the presence of this cluster cannot be taken as a proof that Shakespeare wrote this scene. It is a scene which has not been ascribed to him on other grounds. The cluster, moreover, is incomplete; and though it is only in later plays that the weasel is connected with the drone, we might have ex-

[1] *Shakespeare's Imagination* (1946), p. 184.

pected a reference to sucking. More importantly, the association of *drone, eagle,* and *creeping,* as Armstrong points out, is not peculiar to Shakespeare: it occurs in a popular piece of folk-lore used more than once in Lyly's works:

> There might I behold drones . . . creeping under the wings of a princely eagle, who being carried into her nest, sought there to suck that vein, that would have killed the eagle.

This is closely parallelled in the lines in *Edward III*:

> like the lazy drone
> Crept up by stealth into the Eagle's nest.

There is, moreover, a line in *2 Henry VI* in which this bogus natural history is explicitly repudiated:

> Drones suck not eagles' blood, but rob bee-hives.

Shakespeare might, of course, have put into the mouth of one of his characters something he knew to be absurd; but it seems more likely that he did not write this scene in *Edward III*, and that the appearance of *grudging* and *voluntary* is coincidental, especially as the latter is not used in its musical sense.

The eagle makes a second appearance in the play (III. i. 88), and Miss Bell points out [1] that although there is no mention in this context of the drone there

> is some sort of substitute in the reference to *honey* (80), and to other traces of cluster associations such as *suck forth* (82), *puft with rage* and *gale* (77). Obviously this is not a completely convincing cluster; but it is interesting to notice that

[1] Cf. *op. cit.,* p. 107.

*honey* appears in the Eagle context in *Lucrece* (836) and *Henry V* (I. ii. 187); that both usages in *Edward III* are linked with treachery, poison and snakes (I. i. 104, 116; III. i. 82) while *venom* and *adder* are mentioned in *Lucrece* (850, 871) and treachery is implied in the general drift of the relevant speeches in 2 *Henry VI*; and that references to *colours* (and ships) are found in *Edward III* (I. i. 113, 118; III. i. 68–90), 2 *Henry VI* (IV. i. 97, 114), *Lucrece* (272 *banner*, 279–80) and *Henry V* (I. ii. 164, 192).

It may be added that some of these associations are to be found in other contexts in which eagle is used: *Love's Labours Lost*, IV. iii. 334 *eft, sweet*; *King John*, V. ii. 149 *treachery*; *Richard II*, I. iii. 129 *treachery*; *Richard II*, III. iii. 69 *thunder, lightning, treachery*; *Titus Andronicus*, IV. iv. 83 *honey-stalks*.

Now both these semi-clusters appear in scenes which are not generally ascribed to Shakespeare, and one therefore tends to be suspicious of their validity. Armstrong quite properly warns us not to rely too heavily on clusters as a test of authorship; and these are incomplete and depend on associations not peculiar to Shakespeare. There is, moreover, always the possibility that an anonymous author, steeped, as Swinburne assumes, in the early works of Shakespeare, would unconsciously pick up the same associations.

One other cluster – not one of those analysed by Armstrong – is to be found in *Edward III* (II. i. 146–72). The key-word, *blot*, is accompanied by *heaven, night, moon, constancy, disguise (mask), sovereign, eye, winter,* and *sun*. All these words, except *constancy* and *disguise*, appear also in a passage in *Love's Labour Lost* (IV. iii. 220 ff.); five of them, including *inconstancy*, *constant*, and *disguise*, appear in *The Two Gentlemen of Verona* (V. iv. 107 ff.), seven of them in *Richard II* (I. iii. 202 ff.), six of them in *Venus and Adonis* (773–816), and five in another passage in the same poem (154–93). There are traces of the same cluster in ten other plays and in *Lucrece*.

Apart from image-clusters appearing in several plays, many other passages in *Edward III* have multiple links with single passages in Shakespeare. The pun on *apparelled* and *suit* (II. i. 410–11) reappears in *As You Like It* (IV. i. 88); and in both contexts the pun is closely followed by a mention of a *solicitor* or *attorney*. A few lines later (418–24) the author of *Edward III* has a passage containing *leprous*, *die*, *envenometh*, *dug*, *blood*, and *sin*. This may be compared with the speech of the ghost in *Hamlet* (I. v. 64–75), which contains *leperous distillment*, *blood*, *milk* (cf. *dug*), and *sin*. In the same scene a reference to Sara (II. i. 254) is followed by allusions to *chaplains*, *desire*, *death*, and *marriage*. In *Richard II* (IV. iii. 29–36) a reference to Sara's husband, Abraham, is preceded by a mention of *chaplain* and the other three words.

A few examples may be given of less extended parallels. The pun on *habit*, whether intentional or not, in the line (I. ii. 146) –

Whose habit rude and manners blunt and playne –

may be compared with the juxtaposition in *Hamlet* (I. iv. 29–30) –

by some habit, that too much ore-leauens
The forme of plausiue manners –

with that in *Love's Labour's Lost* (V. ii. 365–8), where the same quibble occurs –

> My Ladie (to the manner of the daies)
> In curtesie giues vndeseruing praise.
> We foure indeed confronted were with foure
> In Russian habit –

and with that in *Twelfth Night* (III. iv. 80–1) –

> the manner how: . . . in the habite of some Sir of note.

The comparison of a face to a book (IV. iv. 128–9; V. i. 3) and the juxtaposition of *face*, *matter*, and *printed* in the lines (IV. v. 26–8) –

> that verie feare in deed,
> Which is so gastly printed in thy face:
> What is the matter? –

may be compared with several passages in Shakespeare –

> Although the Print be little, the whole Matter
> And Coppy of the Father: (Eye, Nose, Lippe,
> The trick of's Frowne . . .)
> (*Winter's Tale*, II. iii. 98–100)

The following lines (IV. iv. 97–8), containing, perhaps, a quibble on *ore* –

> For I will staine my horse quite ore with bloud,
> And double guild my spurs –

may be compared with 'double gild his trebble guilt' (*2 Henry IV*, IV. v. 29), and with Lady Macbeth's deter-

mination to gild the faces of the grooms. A description
in the same scene of *Edward III* (IV. iv. 20–2) –

> pendants cuff the aire
> And beat the windes, that for their gaudinesse
> Struggles to kisse them –

looks forward to a passage in *Macbeth* (I. ii. 50–1) –

> Where the Norweyan Banners flowt the Skie
> And fanne our people cold –

and to the famous description of Cleopatra's first meeting
with Antony (II. ii. 197–201) –

> Purple the Sailes: and so perfumed that
> The Windes were Loue-sicke with them. The Owers were
> Siluer,
> Which to the tune of Flutes kept stroke, and made
> The water which they beate to follow faster;
> As amorous of their strokes. –

and here, as in the *Edward III* passage, there is a lavish
use of gold and silver.

A few more parallels may be mentioned briefly. A
passage in the first scene (I. i. 44–6) may be compared
with one in *Hamlet* (V. ii. 247–9) where the Prince
compliments Laertes. *Fiery* and *ignorance* are common to
both passages, and *rakt* may have suggested *stick*. In the
same scene (I. i. 67) 'occasion laughs' resembles another
*Hamlet* passage (I. iii. 54), 'occasion smiles'. In the next
scene (I. ii. 78–80) there is a striking parallel with *King
Lear* (II. iii. 11); 'bare arms' are common to both passages,
'faceless' suggested 'outface', and 'weather' suggested
'winds'. There is no point in listing parallels with the
*Sonnets* and the early plays, as the author of *Edward III*

may be indebted to Shakespeare in these cases. But as *King John* may have been written later, it may be worth while to record two parallels with that play. A phrase in *Edward III* (IV. iv. 9) 'eielesse terror of all ending night' is paralleled by 'eyeless night' (*King John*, V. vi. 12); and there are seven, not very significant, parallels with an earlier passage (III. ii. 56–71). *Tread, march, fire, son, wives,* and *cities* are to be found here and in *King John* (II. i. 227–41), and *reeking* corresponds to *smoke*.

There remains to be considered the relationship between three Shakespearian plays and *Edward III*. The resemblances between the Countess scenes and the Lady Grey scene in *3 Henry VI* may be due to the fact that the author of *Edward III* was deliberately imitating Shakespeare's early play. The resemblances between the battle scenes of *Edward III* and those of *Henry V* may be explained as the imitation by Shakespeare of a play he had seen, read, or performed.[1] But Angelo's temptation of Isabella offers more substantial grounds for believing that Shakespeare had a hand in the Countess scenes. In both plays a virtuous woman preserved her chastity against the assaults of a ruler. Both heroines attack the abuse of authority. Warwick's 'sentence' about the ape, already quoted above –

> An euill deed, done by authoritie,
> Is sin and subbornation: Decke an Ape
> In tissue, and the beautie of the robe
> Adds but the greater scorne vnto the beast –

[1] Cf. M. C. Bradbrook, *Shakespeare and Elizabethan Poetry* (1951), p. 209; E. Phipson, *N.S.S. Transactions*, pp. 58 ff.; Kittredge's notes on *Henry V*, I. i. 43, I. ii. 245, I. iv. 57, III. vii. 163, IV. Prol. 26.

# Shakespeare's Hand in *Edward III*

appears to have suggested –

> proud man,
> Drest in a little briefe authoritie,
> Most ignorant of what he's most assur'd,
> (His glassie Essence) like an angry Ape
> Plaies such phantastique tricks before high heauen,
> As makes the Angels weepe.

Warwick tells his daughter –

> That sinne doth ten times agreuate it selfe
> That is committed in a holie place –

And Angelo asks himself –

> Shall we desire to raze the Sanctuary
> And pitch our euils there?

Warwick declares that –

> The freshest summers day doth sonnest taint
> The lothed carrion that it seems to kisse:

and Angelo cries –

> but it is I,
> That, lying by the Violet in the Sunne,
> Doe as the Carrion do's, not as the flowre,
> Corrupt with vertuous season.

The Countess speaks of 'the dangerous rein of liberty';
Angelo tells Isabella –

> And now I giue my sensuall race, the reine –

and Claudio declares that his restraint comes from too
much liberty. Finally, the Countess compares counter-
feiting coins with adultery –

## Shakespeare as Collaborator

He that doth clip or counterfeit your stamp
Shall die, my Lord; and will your sacred selfe
Comit high treason against the King of heauen,
To stamp his Image in forbidden mettel,
Forgetting your alleagance and your othe?

Angelo similarly declares –

It were as good
To pardon him, that hath from nature stolne
A man already made, as to remit
Their sawcie sweetnes, that do coyne heauens Image
In stamps that are forbid.

Of this last parallel Swinburne declared that 'men of Shakespeare's stamp ... do not thus repeat themselves'. Certainly Shakespeare, having written the *Measure for Measure* passage, would not later produce the inferior version of *Edward III*; but if, as is generally agreed, the passage in *Edward III* was written first, it would be in accordance with Shakespeare's usual custom for him to refine on a passage he had written earlier. Hundreds of examples could be given of similar recurrences in plays whose authenticity no one disputes; and in nearly every case the second version is more pregnant and impressive than the first. Sometimes, as here, the earlier passage reveals the process by which Shakespeare evolved the later image. In the same way the speeches of Audley and Prince in IV. iv. seem to contain the germ of the Duke's great speech (III. i.) and of Claudio's reply –

For, from the instant we begin to liue
We do pursue and hunt the time to die: . . .
If, then, we hunt for death, why do we feare it? . . .
I will not giue a pennie for a lyfe . . .
Since for to liue is but to seeke to die,
And dying but beginning of new lyfe.

Meerely, thou art deaths foole,
For him thou labourest by thy flight to shun,
And yet runst toward him still . . .
To sue to liue, I finde I seeke to die,
And seeking death, finde life.

Of course, even if these parallels are valid and not the expression of commonplaces, Shakespeare might conceivably be echoing and improving on a play by another dramatist, in which, perhaps, he had himself acted. But if this were so, it would be unique in his career; for even where he was using a play as a direct source, as he did in writing *King Lear*, there are comparatively few verbal echoes.

The tests we have applied to *Edward III* are not, perhaps, conclusive. Hart's vocabulary tests indicate the possibility of the Shakespearian authorship of the whole play; and these are supported by the somewhat ambiguous evidence offered by Miss Mary Bell. But the test of the incidence of new words appears to support the view of double authorship. Although iterative imagery has been found in Marlowe, and although it is present in the work of Webster and other Jacobean dramatists, Shakespeare, as far as we know, was the only poet using it between the death of Marlowe and December 1595.

Although some unknown dramatist [1] might have used iterative imagery, its distribution in the different scenes would support the theory that this dramatist was mainly responsible for the Countess scenes and IV. iv. Two inconclusive image-clusters are to be found in the scenes not usually ascribed to Shakespeare; but other clusters, which appear to be less ambiguous, are to be found in the 'Shakespearian' scenes. There are many parallels between these scenes and genuine plays of Shakespeare, including plays written after *Edward III*, and the scenes contain some of Shakespeare's characteristic mannerisms. The strongest argument for Shakespeare's authorship of part of the play is the presence of close parallels with *Henry V* and *Measure for Measure*. If Shakespeare had no hand in the play he was at least intimately acquainted with it, more intimately than with any known Elizabethan play. One theory which would cover all the facts – and it is difficult to think of another that would – is that Shakespeare, as in *Pericles*, was hastily revising a play by another dramatist, certain scenes being entirely rewritten, and the remainder being left with comparatively few alterations.

[1] S. R. Golding, *N.Q.* cliv, p. 313, argues that *Edward III* was written by the same author as *A Larum for London*. Only one of his parallels seems to be significant, and it can be explained as the imitation of one dramatist by the other.

# *Edward III*

English history provided the plots of many Elizabethan plays. But readers of Mr Irving Ribner's recent survey of the subject are likely to feel that, apart from Marlowe's *Edward II* at the beginning of the period and Ford's belated masterpiece, *Perkin Warbeck*, a generation later, there are no English history plays written by Shakespeare's contemporaries which are worth reading for their own sake. They were, for the most part, written by hack writers to satisfy a public demand – a demand aroused perhaps both by the sense of national pride which resulted from the defeat of the Spanish Armada and by the tireless efforts of Tudor propagandists. The historical matter, moreover, was easily available in Stow, Holinshed, Hall, Froissart, and other chroniclers, and this must have been a consideration to poorly paid writers, pressed for time and anxious to satisfy the public's voracious demands for new plays.

*Edward III*, whoever wrote it, is a much more impressive play than Peele's *Edward I* or *The Famous Victories of Henry V* or *The Troublesome Raigne of King John* – even when allowances have been made for the bad texts of those plays. It was planned as a whole; or at least the authors (if there were two) worked in collaboration,

using the same sources, and taking care to link the
Countess scenes with the rest of the play. The King in
Act II looks forward to his French campaign:

> Away, loose silkes of wavering vanity!
> Shall the large limmit of fair Britannye
> By me be overthrowne? and shall I not
> Master this little mansion of my selfe?
> Give me an Armor of eternall steele;
> I go to conquer kings.

In the next act the King of France refers to Edward's
pursuit of the Countess:

> For whats this Edward, but a belly god,
> A tender and lasciuious wantonnes,
> That th'other day was almost dead for loue?

Not only are the two sections of the play linked together
in this way, but even the war scenes are competently
written. It seems probable, however, that the play was
written by Shakespeare in collaboration, for some scenes
one would be unwilling to ascribe to him at any period
of his career – not because they are bad, but because their
badness is unlike Shakespeare's. The very first scene may
be taken as an example. It was probably imitated from
*The Famous Victories*, and for this reason resembles the
first scene in *Henry V*; but the badness of the latter seems
to be due to Shakespeare's attempt to turn into verse an
intractable passage of Holinshed about the Salic law,
while the badness of the *Edward III* passage is absolute.
As in *Henry V* and *The Famous Victories*, the exposition in

*Edward III* is followed immediately by the arrival of the French ambassador. Warwick's lines –

> Byd him leaue off the Lyon's case he weares;
> Lest, meeting with the Lyon in the field,
> He chaunce to teare him peece-meale for his pride –

were probably suggested either by *The Troublesome Raigne* or by *King John* itself. The blank verse of this scene is monotonous, and nearly all end-stopped, only a line here and there being at all memorable. One line –

> See, how occasion laughes me in the face! –

is reminiscent of one in *Hamlet* –

> Occasion smiles upon a second leave.

One image happens to fit in with the group of masking images which (as I have shown) is characteristic of the Shakespearian parts of the play; but this is probably accidental.

The Countess of Salisbury is introduced in the second scene; and though the Shakespearian portion is generally thought to begin at l. 95, the earlier part is much better written than the first scene. There are a number of fine lines, as for example the one describing the bagpipes which

> Bray foorth their Conquest, and our ouerthrow,
> Euen in the barraine, bleake, and fruitlesse aire.

There is a more sustained passage in which King David boasts:

And neuer shall our bonny riders rest;
Nor rusting canker haue the time to eate
Their light-borne snaffles, nor their nimble spurres;
Nor lay aside their Iacks of Gymould mayle;
Nor hang their staues of grayned Scottish ash
In peacefull wise vpon their citie wals;
Nor from their buttoned tawny leatherne belts
Dismisse their byting whinyards, – till your King
Cry out: *Enough, spare England now for pittie!*

The early part of the scene, before King Edward's entrance, is lively and amusing. The dividing of the spoil by the Scots before they have captured Roxborough Castle is nicely contrasted with their precipitate flight on the approach of the English forces; and the Countess's fliting of the cowardly braggarts is spirited and effective. But although it would be difficult to tell from the verse alone that this was not by the same author as the later part of the scene, it might be argued that the undaunted woman therein depicted does not quite harmonize with Warwick's description of her a few lines later as one

whose beauty tyrant feare,
As a May blossome with pernitious winds,
Hath sullied, withered, ouercast, and donne.

The rest of the scene, appropriately enough, is written in a more lyrical style, the last forty lines being in rhymed couplets, and some of the imagery recalling that of the *Sonnets, Romeo and Juliet,* and *Love's Labour's Lost.*

Now, in the Sunne alone it doth not lye,
With light to take light from a mortall eye;
For here two day stars that mine eies would see,
More then the Sunne steales myne owne light from mee ...

Let not thy presence, like the Aprill sunne,
Flatter our earth and sodenly be done ...

For where the golden Ore doth buried lie,
The ground, vndeckt with natures tapestrie,
Seemes barrayne, sere, vnfertill, fructless, dry;
And where the vpper turfe of earth doth boast
His pide perfumes and party-colloured cost,
Delue there, and find this issue and their pride
To spring from ordure and corruptions side.
But to make vp my all too long compare,
These ragged walles no testimonie are,
What is within; but, like a cloake, doth hide
From weathers Waste the vnder garnisht pride.

These last lines, spoken by the Countess, are not particularly in character; but they are intended to show that
she is intelligent as well as beautiful, and thus go some
way to justify the King's infatuation:

> As wise, as faire; what fond fit can be heard,
> When wisedome keepes the gate as beuties gard?

The whole of the second act is devoted to the King's
unsuccessful attempt on the Countess's chastity. It resembles in some ways the scene in *3 Henry VI* in which
Edward IV's advances to Lady Grey are repelled so that
he is constrained to offer marriage, but it is altogether

more serious and mature in its treatment of the theme. The conversation between Edward IV and Lady Grey, observed from a distance by Clarence and Gloucester, is carried on for the most part in single-line speeches:

> *K. Edw.* No, by my troth, I did not mean such love.
> *L. Grey.* Why, then you mean not as I thought you did.
> *K. Edw.* To tell thee plain, I aim to lie with thee.
> *L. Grey.* To tell you plain, I had rather lie in prison.
> *K. Edw.* Why, then thou shalt not have thy husband's lands.
> *L. Grey.* Why, then mine honesty shall be my dower.

This stychomythia is expertly managed, but the effect is inevitably artificial. The verse offers room neither for development of character nor of argument, nor for the use of imagery. The situation is reduced to its lowest terms – Virtuous Woman rejects Lustful Monarch, who is converted to the idea of matrimony. The second act of *Edward III* is much longer and more complex; the author has plenty of room to develop situation and character; the King's temptation is not as blunt and crude as Edward IV's had been, the guilty love being tempered by poetry; and both the King and the Countess are furnished with long and eloquent speeches. The King, moreover, makes use of Lodowick and the Countess's father, Warwick, to weaken her resistance.

Algernon Charles Swinburne, who analysed the scene in some detail, but not without prejudice, convinced himself that Shakespeare had no hand in it. Some of his arguments are difficult to take seriously. He appears to have been outraged by the character of Lodowick, whom he described as poet and pimp. The indignation comes a little oddly from Swinburne, who was fresh from the composition of *Poems and Ballads* and who was even then meditating his great poem on adulterous love, *Tristram in Lyonesse*. Nor is the moral character of the poets depicted in Shakespeare's acknowledged plays so lofty that we can assume that Lodowick's portrayal is beneath him. The time-serving poet in *Timon of Athens* [1] and the lynched poet in *Julius Caesar* are neither idealized; and Sir Thurio is advised by Proteus to

> lay lime to tangle her desires
> By wailful sonnets, whose composed rhymes
> Shall be full-fraught with serviceable vows.

Lodowick is not a professional poet; he is a lord, the King's friend and confidant. He is full of admiration for the Countess's beauty before he is asked to compose a poem to express the King's love. This is made clear by the soliloquy in which he compares the King's blushes to hers:

> His cheekes put on their scarlet ornaments;
> But no more like her oryentall red,
> Then Bricke to Corrall or liue things to dead.

It should also be noted that although Lodowick doubtless guesses to whom his poem is to be sent, the King does

---

[1] But I have argued (*Essays in Criticism*, III, pp. 120–1) that the poet in *Timon of Athens* was not as bad as he is usually painted.

not tell him; and that the lines he composes serve only to remind the King of the Countess's chastity:

> More faire and chast then is the queen of shades,
> More bould in constancie then Iudith was.

If Lodowick were a pimp he would be a singularly ineffective one, and a disgrace to his profession. It is surely more reasonable to suppose that he is an honest man who does his best to deter the King from his adulterous passion, and that he does not deserve the hard things said of him by Swinburne.

The temptation of the Countess may be divided into four sections. In the first, after a soliloquy by the King, he asks Lodowick to write a poem in praise of his unnamed mistress, but he decides finally that only a lover can write of love (II. i. 25–183). In the second section the King makes his first proposal to the Countess, who assumes, or pretends to assume, that he is testing her virtue (184–276). In the third section the King tricks Warwick into pleading for him, and the Countess, to her father's joy, repels his advocacy (277–459). In the fourth section the King, on seeing his son, momentarily repents; but he again presses his suit on the entrance of the Countess. She shames him into repentance by threatening to stab herself, but not before he has offered to murder the Queen and the Countess's husband (II. ii. 1–211).

The four sections exhibit a rising tension from the King's opening soliloquy, through the Countess's first repulse of his suit, and the tragic dilemma of her father, to the final impassioned argument culminating in the threat of violence. The only dramatic objection to this act is that the remaining three acts of the play are something of an anti-climax, not merely because they are generally inferior in style, but because the qualities they possess are epic rather than dramatic.

Tucker Brooke, who regarded the unknown author of *Edward III* as 'one of the truest poets of his generation', nevertheless complained of the 'rather cloying sweetness' and 'quibbling mawkishness' of the Countess scenes. The date of the play is not known, but it is likely to have been written after 1593 – because of its allusion to *Lucrece* – and it must certainly have been written before December 1595, when it was entered in the Stationers' Register. If one reads Elizabethan plays – even *Romeo and Juliet* and *Richard II* – written during these years one can find many passages which could as justly be dismissed as 'cloying sweetness' and 'quibbling mawkishness'. But the sweetness is not cloying to all readers; the quibble was an admired grace of style used by Shakespeare throughout his life and not deserving the contempt with which it was treated by critics from Dryden to Bradley; and the mawkishness is a matter of opinion.

The dialogue between the King and Lodowick is interesting for a number of reasons. One, the misjudged character of Lodowick, I have already mentioned. A second is the fact that the King is given better poetry to speak when he is instructing Lodowick on the theme of the poem he wants him to write than the poem itself. Thirdly, the lines provide an interesting account of how an Elizabethan poet set to work, and it may possibly reflect the author's own habits of composition.

The King states, though not in so many words, that the

function of poetry – of the poet when inspired by a 'golden muse' – is to express emotion and to arouse a similar emotion in a reader. Then he complains of the inadequacy of language to express the praises of his mistress, a theme touched on in the *Sonnets* and in *Love's Labour's Lost*:

> Better then bewtifull thou must begin,
> Deuise for faire a fairer word then faire,
> And euery ornament that thou wouldest praise,
> Fly it a pitch aboue the soare of praise.

The King then makes a kind of inventory of his mistress's qualities – her rank, her voice, her hair, her eyes – in a way which corresponds to the favourite method of Elizabethan sonneteers. But the inventory is complicated by the King's own objections to his comparisons. He compares the Countess's voice to that of the nightingale, and then recalls the danger of referring to the story of Philomel:

> The nightingale singes of adulterate wrong,
> And that, compared, is too satyrical.

Or, in comparing her hair to various things –

> Her hair, far softer then the silke wormes twist,
> Like to a flattering glas, doth make more faire
> The yelow Amber –

he realizes that the comparison can be used more appropriately elsewhere:

> *like a flattering glas*
> Comes in too soone; for, writing of her eies,
> Ile say that like a glas they catch the sunne,
> And thence the hot reflection doth rebounde
> Against my brest, and burnes my hart within.

40

When the Countess appears the King tricks her into swearing to do all she can to remedy his discontent, and then demands her love in fulfilment of her vow. She fails at first to understand him, and this inevitably leads to the quibbling of which Tucker Brooke complained; but when she does understand she rebukes him with a dignity which never violates the respect due to her sovereign.

> But that your lippes were sacred (O) my Lord,
> You would prophane the holie name of loue.

She accuses him of wishing to commit high treason against the king of heaven,

> To stamp his Image in forbidden mettel,
> Forgetting your alleageance and your othe,

and she concludes that he must be testing her virtue on behalf of her husband. The first round goes to her. The author preserves a nice balance of sympathies. Although we are made to approve wholeheartedly of the Countess's virtue, which is never allowed to seem priggish, we are never in danger of thinking that King Edward is a villain. He is intermittently aware of the sinfulness of his conduct, recognizing her words as 'sweet chaplaines to her bewtie' and wishing he

> were a honie-gathering bee,
> To beare the combe of virtue from this flower,
> And not a poison-sucking enuious spider,
> To turn the iuce I take to deadlie venom!

His adulterous love, inspired as it is by the Countess's virtues as well as by her physical attractions, is not as

uncompromisingly evil as the overpowering lust of
Angelo, who is attracted likewise by the virtues of Isabella.

The next stage in the pursuit of the Countess is the
employment of her father as unwilling pandar. The
method employed by the King to achieve this end is a
repetition of his opening gambit with the Countess. He
tricks Warwick into swearing that he will buy the King's
ease even with the loss of his own honour, and then asks
him to persuade his daughter to commit adultery. The
dialogue at this point is closely knit and closely argued,
the King pressing his points home with deliberate am-
biguities, and by seizing on Warwick's admissions. After
he has sworn, for example, the King asks:

> What office were it, to suggest a man
> To breake a lawfull and religious vowe?

Warwick replies:

> An office for the deuill, not for man.

And the King immediately pounces:

> That deuilles office must thou do for me.

If Warwick were given time to think, he would realize
that his own vow was not lawful and religious, and that
he could not properly be bound by it. But his daughter
appears while he is still staggering under the King's re-
quest. The way in which he is torn between his feelings
of loyalty to the King and his sense of right and honour
is neatly indicated both in the soliloquy and in the scene

which follows. Alternate lines in the soliloquy counteract
the lines which precede them:

> Ile say, she must forget her husband Salisbury,
> If she remember to embrace the king;
> Ile say, an othe may easily be broken,
> But not so easily pardoned, being broken;
> Ile say, it is true charitie to loue,
> But not true loue to be so charitable;
> Ile say, his greatnes may beare out the shame,
> But not his kingdome may beare out the sinne;
> Ile say, it is my duety to perswade,
> But not her honestie to giue consent.

So he prefixes his solicitation of his daughter with a warn-
ing which will put her on her guard:

> I am not Warwike, as thou thinkst I am,
> But an atturnie from the Court of hell,
> That thus haue housd my spirite in his forme,
> To do a message to thee from the king.

His argument that she should consent to the King's proposal is continually checked by references to honour,
shame, and 'the bitter potion of reproch'; and he concludes his speech by admitting that he has

> Apparaled sin in vertuous sentences.

When the Countess scornfully repudiates his arguments,
declaring that she will die rather than consent to the
King's 'gracelesse lust', Warwick strengthens her resolu-
tion by retracting what he has said and giving her a series

of sentences on the other side of the question. This speech, which includes a line from one of Shakespeare's *Sonnets*, is the best poetry in the play:

> The freshest summers day doth soonest taint
> The lothed carrion that it seemes to kiss: ...
> That sinne doth ten times agreuate it selfe
> That is committed in a holie place:
> An euill deed, done by authoritie,
> Is sin and subbornation: Decke an Ape
> In tissue, and the beautie of the robe
> Adds but the greater scorne vnto the beast.
> A spatious field of reasons could I vrge
> Betweene his glorie, daughter, and thy shame:
> That poyson showes worst in a golden cup;
> Darke night seemes darker by the lightning flash;
> Lillies that fester smel far worse then weeds;
> And euery glory that inclynes to sin,
> The shame is treble by the opposite.

In the following scene, the conflict in the King's mind is well suggested by his slip of the tongue when he tells Derby in reference to the Emperor's letters –

Ile looke vpon the Countesse minde anone –

and by his almost hysterical annoyance when he hears the sound of a drum. He threatens to use the parchment as his writing-paper, and to hang the drummer in the braces of his drum unless he learns to play the lute. When Prince Edward enters, the resemblance of the boy to his mother corrects the King's 'straid desire' and makes him decide to sail for France; but the announcement that the Countess

'with a smiling cheere' desires access to him makes him
suppose that she is about to surrender:

> That verie smile of hers
> Hath ransomed captiue Fraunce.

The Countess smiles because she has made up her mind
what to do. She turns the tables on the King by doing
with him what he had previously done with her and with
her father. She exacts a vow from him that he will remove
the hindrances between his love and hers. Not realizing
the implications of the vow, the King duly swears; and
the Countess demands the death of her husband and of
the Queen. She hopes by this to shame the King to
repentance; but instead he agrees to their deaths, swearing
that he will outdo Leander by swimming through a
Hellespont of blood, and blaming the Countess's beauty
for his intended crimes. To which the Countess replies:

> O periurde beautie, more corrupted Iudge!
> When to the great Starre-chamber ore our heads
> The vniuersall Sessions cals to count
> This packing euill, we both shall tremble for it.

Finally, she produces two daggers and threatens to commit suicide unless he swears to abandon his unholy suit.
The King again swears, and this time his repentance is
permanent. Awakening from his 'idle dreame', he sets
out immediately for his French campaign. As he has now
mastered his passions, he can proceed to the lesser
victories of war.

The rest of the play is concerned with the sea-battle off
the coast of Flanders and the land-battles of Crecy and

Poitiers. The sea-battle is described by a French sailor in two long messenger speeches, inspired partly, we may suspect, by the defeat of the Spanish Armada, though it is the English fleet which is described as

> Figuring the horned Circle of the Moone.

Although the speeches are not without some vivid touches, the blank verse is stiff, unvaried, and mostly end-stopped, and the imagery is conventional. The ensigns are described as

> Like to a meddow full of sundry flowers,
> Adornes the naked bosome of the earth.

The flagships are compared to fiery dragons. The sea pouring through leaks is described in stilted phrase:

> As did her gushing moysture breake into
> The crannied cleftures of the through shot planks.

And the effect of the cannon-balls is described in a somewhat inappropriate simile:

> Heere flew a head, disseuered from the tronke,
> There mangled armes and legs were tost aloft,
> As when a wherle winde takes the Summer dust
> And scatters it in middle of the aire.

The author is striving hard for epic grandeur, but achieves it only at moments. The best touch is provided by the arrival of the white-faced messenger to announce the defeat, and King John asks:

> Say, mirror of pale death,
> To whome belongs the honor of this day?

46

The remainder of the third act is taken up with the long speeches of invective exchanged between the French and English kings, the ceremonial arming of Prince Edward, and the battle of Crecy, in which the English forces are victorious, largely through the personal valour of the Prince. The writing of these scenes is competent, but undistinguished. In the fourth act we are introduced somewhat belatedly to the Earl of Salisbury, who has reinstated Lord Mountford as Duke of Brittany. He makes no reference in this or later scenes to his Countess, the heroine of the second act: and this is a slight indication that the scenes in which he appears were not by the same author. The Salisbury scenes are concerned largely with a little drama of military honour, as the Countess scenes had been concerned with marital honour. Salisbury releases Villiers without a ransom on condition he procures him a safe-conduct to Calais. Villiers swears that if he fails to obtain the passport from Charles, Duke of Normandy, he will return to Salisbury as his prisoner. When he arrives at the French camp Charles refuses the passport, and Villiers tells him he must return to prison. Charles thinks his scruples are absurd, and there ensues the following passage of dialogue:

*Vil.*  Ah, but it is mine othe, my gratious Lord,
      Which I in conscience may not violate,
      Or else a kingdome should not draw me hence.
*Ch.*  Thine othe? why, that doth bind thee to abide:
      Hast thou not sworne obedience to thy Prince?
*Vil.*  In all things that vprightly he commands:
      But either to perswade or threaten me,

> Not to performe the couenant of my word,
> Is lawlesse, and I need not to obey.
>
> *Ch.* Why, is it lawfull for a man to kill,
> And not to breake a promise with his foe?
>
> *Vil.* To kill, my Lord, when warre is once proclaymd,
> So that our quarrel be for wrongs receaude,
> No doubt is lawfully permitted vs:
> But in an othe we must be well aduisd,
> How we do sweare, and, when we once haue sworne,
> Not to infringe it, though we die therefore:
> Therefore, my Lord, as willing I returne,
> As if I were to flie to paradise.

The way in which one's obedience to a prince is limited by the over-riding moral law links up with the problem confronting Warwick and the Countess in the second act; and just as King Edward is converted by the Countess, Charles is converted by the virtue of Villiers. Armed with safe-conduct so procured, Salisbury is captured by the French forces; and King John forthwith orders him to be hanged on the nearest tree. Charles, infected with Villiers' sense of honour, protests hotly:

> I hope your highnes will not so disgrace me,
> And dash the vertue of my seale at armes:
> He hath my neuer broken name to shew,
> Carectred with this princely hande of mine;
> And rather let me leaue to be a prince
> Than break the stable verdict of a prince:
> I doo beseech you, let him passe in quiet.

King John tells him that he can overrule any promise made by one of his subjects; and Charles exclaims bitterly:

48

> What, am I not a soldier in my word?
> Then, armes, adieu, and let them fight that list!
> Shall I not giue my girdle from my wast,
> But with a gardion I shall be controld,
> To saie I may not giue my things awaie?
> Vpon my soule, had Edward, prince of Wales,
> Ingagde his word, writ downe his noble hand
> For all your knights to passe his fathers land,
> The roiall king, to grace his warlike sonne,
> Would not alone safe conduct giue to them,
> But with all bountie feasted them and theirs.

Just as Charles had been converted by Villiers, so King John is shamed into allowing Salisbury to go free.

The Crecy scenes have been praised by Tucker Brooke for their verve and exhilaration, and they are certainly exciting. The arming of the Prince, the King's refusal to send aid, the despair of his friends who think him doomed, and his triumphant entrance form an obviously effective sequence of incidents; but the actual poetry is disappointing. The imagery is perfunctory at times, and at other times laboured, as when the Prince compares his fight to a voyage:

> And now, behold, after my winters' toyle,
> My payneful voyage on the boystrous sea
> Of warres deuouring gulphes and steely rocks,
> I bring my fraught vnto the wished port,
> My Summers hope, my trauels sweet reward.

Some of the verse, moreover, is extremely feeble:

> Let Edward be deliuered by our hands,
> And still, in danger, hele expect the like:
> But if himselfe himselfe redeeme from thence,

## Shakespeare as Collaborator

> He wil haue vanquisht cheerefull death and feare,
> And euer after dread their force no more
> Then if they were but babes or Captiue slaues.

The Poitiers scenes, on the other hand, reach and maintain a much higher poetic and dramatic level. They resemble in many ways the Agincourt scenes in *Henry V*. In both the English forces, heavily outnumbered, are in an apparently hopeless situation. In both the French are gorgeously arrayed and over-confident, though in *Edward III* they are depicted more sympathetically. There is real splendour in Audley's description of the French army, and the successive heralds who demand surrender, bring a horse so that the Black Prince may escape, and finally offer a prayer-book so that he may prepare his mind for death, not merely characterize the French, but enable the Prince to exhibit a notable courage in the face of death. Henry V never loses hope, but the Black Prince accepts what he regards as the certainty of defeat and death.

> Audley, the armes of death embrace vs round,
> And comfort haue we none, saue that to die
> We pay sower earnest for a sweeter life.

These lines occur at the beginning of one of the best scenes in the play. The description of the French army whose

> new-replenisht pendants cuff the aire
> And beat the windes, that for their gaudinesse
> Struggles to kisse them:

which rises to a climax in the lines –

> And on the Hill behind stands certaine death
> In pay and seruice with Chattillion –

and the image used by the Prince when he asks Audley
for consolation in the face of death –

> Thy selfe art bruis'd and bit with many broiles,
> And stratagems forepast with yron pens
> Are texted in thine honorable face;
> Thou art a married man in this distresse,
> But danger wooes me as a blushing maide:
> Teach me an answere to this perilous time. –

are excellent; but other lines in the same scene are so
feeble, that one is driven to suspect corruption in the
text. Just before the lines just quoted, for example, the
Prince is made to say:

> Now, Audley, sound those siluer winges of thine,
> And let those milke-white messengers of time
> Shew thy times learning in this dangerous time.

This confused passage in which Audley's white hair is
apparently compared to the white plumage of an angel,
and his voice to the beating of an angel's wings, is unlikely to have been written by the same poet in that form.
The repetition of *time* at the end of a line suggests that
the confusion may be due to the compositor.

Audley's speech of consolation, as we saw above, reads
like a rough draft for the Duke's advice to Claudio, as the
Prince's reply resembles Claudio's. Audley says:

> For, from the instant we begin to liue,
> We do pursue and hunt the time to die: ...
> If, then, we hunt for death, why do we feare it?
> If we feare it, why do we follow it?

## Shakespeare as Collaborator

The Prince exclaims:

> Ah, what an idiot hast thou made of lyfe,
> To seeke the thing it feares! and how disgrast
> The imperiall victorie of murdring death, . . .
> I will not giue a pennie for a lyfe,
> Nor halfe a halfpennie to shun grim death,
> Since for to liue is but to seeke to die,
> And dying but beginning of new lyfe.
> Let come the houre when he that rules it will!
> To liue or die I hold indifferent.

The two other scenes relating to Audley also contain some superb passages, and the poorer parts there are due to the lapses of the author rather than to those of the compositor. Audley is mortally wounded, and he is asked how he fares. He replies:

> Euen as a man may do
> That dines at such a bloudie feast as this.

He asks his squires to carry him to the Prince,

> That in the crimson brauerie of my bloud
> I may become him with saluting him.

The Prince, on seeing him, says:

> Speake, thou that wooest death with thy careless smile,
> As if thou wert enamored of thyne end:
> What hungry sword hath so bereaud thy face,
> And lopt a true friend from my louing soule?

The first two lines are magnificent, the others a sad anti-climax; and when the Prince continues with absurd

bombast it is difficult to understand how so good a poet
could be guilty of such lines:

> If thou wilt drinke the blood of captyue kings,
> Or that it were restoritiue, command
> A Health of kings blood, and Ile drinke to thee.

A moment later the poet recovers himself, giving Audley
the splendid, if over-rhetorical, lines:

> If I could hold dym death but at a bay,
> Till I did see my liege thy royall father,
> My soule should yeeld this Castle of my flesh,
> To darkenes, consummation, dust, and Wormes.

It would appear that the author of these scenes was a
young poet, 'able to bombast out a blank verse as the
best' of the University Wits, as Greene said of Shakespeare, but liable to strange lapses; one whose sense of
situation was superior to his power of characterization.

In the last act the incident of the burghers of Calais is
dealt with in a very perfunctory way. It is followed by
the arrival of Copland with King David of Scotland, Copland's attitude to his prisoner resembling that of Hotspur
in *1 Henry IV*. The rest of the scene is taken up with a long
speech of Salisbury describing what he thinks is the
defeat of the Black Prince at Poitiers, followed by the
arrival of the victorious Prince with his French prisoners.
As the audience already know the result of the battle, the
effect of the contrast is somewhat spoilt; but it serves to
remind us of the way in which victory had been snatched
from the jaws of certain defeat.

*Edward III* as a whole is not an entirely satisfying play.

The first two acts, in spite of the links to which we have called attention, are not sufficiently related to the remaining three. Critics have shown that the King, by conquering himself, makes himself worthy to conquer France; and the Salisbury–Villiers scenes provide us with an *exemplum* of military honour to set beside the *exemplum* of marital honour in the Countess scenes. Both of them, moreover, define the limitations of a subject's obedience. But there is, nevertheless, a switch of interest. Of the three main characters in the first two acts only King Edward appears in the second half of the play, and there his role is subordinated to that of his son, the hero of Crecy and Poitiers. The play, therefore, seems to fall between two kinds. There is enough attempt at unity to make it fit uneasily into the class of chronicle plays, but not enough unity is achieved to allow it to rank with the History play as developed by Marlowe and Shakespeare.

Tucker Brooke ascribed the whole play to Peele. Comparison with his other plays is difficult because only *The Arraignment of Paris* exists in an adequate text. The opening lines of *David and Bethsabe* are as fine in their way as anything in *Edward III*, but the way is quite different. *Edward I* is much nearer to *Edward III* in theme, but its style is more Marlovian, and it contains few sustained passages of poetry. Tucker Brooke suggests that *Edward III*, although finer than any of Peele's known works, was potentially within his grasp:

> A few more years of practice, a free hand, and the change from the dry threshed husks of Biblical narrative to the full and stimulating garners of native history might have performed a far greater transfiguration.

The dates of Peele's other plays are mostly uncertain, but some of them were probably written no earlier than *Edward III*. Nothing we know of his career suggests that he would in his later years have had the opportunity of escaping from the unsatisfactory conditions of a hack-writer, or of rising so far above his accustomed level. If Peele had a hand in the play we might explain its characteristics by an hypothesis similar to the one advanced by some critics concerning *Titus Andronicus* – that Shakespeare revised a play by Peele, rewriting the Countess scenes, and making extensive alterations in Act IV. But critics of Elizabethan drama have a tendency to ascribe to Peele any anonymous plays of the period for which no suitable author can be found; and the evidence for his hand in *Edward III* is very slight.

## IV

# Shakespeare's Hand in *Pericles*

When I first wrote on the relationship of Wilkins' novel, *The Painfull Aduentures of Pericles*, and the Shakespearian play, I pointed out that it was still a matter of controversy: [1]

> Some critics imagine that the novel was based on the play; others think that the play was based on the novel; and Dugdale Sykes argued forcibly that Wilkins based a play on the novel he had himself written, and that the last three acts of this play were afterwards revised by Shakespeare.

Since these words were written the situation has changed. No one, for reasons which will be apparent, now thinks that the play was based on the novel, and no one thinks that Wilkins based a play on the novel he had himself written, and that Shakespeare revised the last three acts of this play. The republication of *The Painfull Aduentures*, with detailed references to its relationship to the play,[2] the publication of Mr J. C. Maxwell's edition (in the New Cambridge Shakespeare), and, above all, the publication of Mr Philip Edwards' article [3] in *Shakespeare Survey 5* have

[1] *English Studies*, XXX (1949), p. 5.
[2] ed. K. Muir (Liverpool University Press, 1953).
[3] pp. 25–49.

altered the nature of the controversy. What is now at issue is whether Wilkins' novel was based on Shakespeare's play, or on the Ur-*Pericles*, the hypothetical source of it. The difference between the first two acts and the last three Mr Edwards ascribes to the differing habits of two reporters: [1]

> These two work by quite different methods: the first welds into mediocre verse the words, phrases and general sense of the original so far as he can remember them. He is at his best in prose, where remodelling is not attempted. The second reporter, perhaps giving the original very much more faithfully than his predecessor, makes no attempt at rewriting, and after the first scene does not make more than desultory attempts to write down the verse in lines.

Mr Edwards, it should be added, gives good reasons for thinking that this reported text was set up by three compositors, and that all three were concerned with both parts of the play. It can therefore be deduced that the difference between the two parts cannot be ascribed to the differing competence of the compositors.

It may be freely admitted that Mr Edwards has made out his case that there were three compositors. The theory that there were two reporters is less certain, and before we discuss the question it will be as well to dispose of a minor question – the relationship of Wilkins' novel to Twine's.

Twine's *Patterne of Painefull Aduentures* had been reissued in 1607, and it is not difficult to demonstrate that whatever use Wilkins made of a *Pericles* play he had

[1] p. 45.

Twine's tale in front of him as he wrote, and that he cheerfully lifted not merely phrases but whole sentences and paragraphs from it with very little verbal alteration. I have listed in my edition of Wilkins' novel some seventy borrowings from Twine, and though a few of these may have been common to Twine and the play (as performed), the great majority were taken direct from Twine. One example may be given by one of the more substantial borrowings: [1]

| Twine | Wilkins |
|---|---|
| But hearken unto me, and I will declare unto thee the beginning of thy birth, to the intent thou mayst know how to guide thy selfe after my death. Apollonius, the prince of Tyrus, is thy father, and Lucina, king Altistrates daughter, was thy mother; who, being in travell with thee, died after thou wast borne, and thy father, Apollonius, inclosed her bodie in a chest, with princely ornaments, laying twenty talents of gold at her head, and as much at her feete in silver, with a scedule written, and threw the chest overboard into the sea, that whether soever it were driven, it might suffice to burie her, according to her estate. Thus wast thou born upon the sea; and | But hearken vnto me, and I will declare vnto thee the beginning of thy birth, that thou mayest knowe how to guide thy selfe after my death: *Pericles*, the Prince of *Tyre* is thy father, and *Thaysa* king *Symonides* daughter was thy mother: which father and mother departed from thy grandsir at *Pentapolis* toward their kingdom of *Tyre*, thy mother being at Sea, fell in trauell with thee, and died after thou wert borne: when thy Father *Pericles* inclosed her body in a Chest with princely ornaments, laying twenty talents of golde at her head, and as much at her feete in siluer: with a Scedule written, containing the dignitie of her birth, and maner of her death, then caused the Chest to be thrown ouer-boorde into the Sea, thorow a superstitious opinion which the mariners beleeued, leauing her body so inriched, to the intent, that |

[1] Wilkins, pp. 69–71.

thy fathers ship, with much wrestling of contrarie windes, and with his unspeakeable griefe of minde, arriued at this shoare, and brought thee in thy swadling clothes unto this citie, where hee with great care delivered thee unto this thine hoste Stranguilo and Dionisiades his wife, to be fostered up diligently, and left me heere also to attend upon thee. Moreover, he sware an othe, that he would not poule his head, clip his beard, nor pare his nayles, untill he had married thee unto some man at ripe yeares.

whither soeuer it were driuen, they that found it, in regarde of the riches, would bury her according to her estate. Thus Lady were you borne vppon the waters, and your fathers Ship with much wrestling of contrary windes, and with his vnspeakeable griefe of minde, arriued at this shoare, and brought thee in thy swadling clowtes vnto this Citty, where he with great care deliuered thee vnto this thine hoste *Cleon* and *Dyonysa* his wife, diligently to be fostered vp, and left me heere also to attend vppon thee, swearing this oath to keepe inuiolate, his haire should be vncisserd, his face vntrimmed, himselfe in all things vncomely continually to mourne for your dead mother, vntill your ripe yeares gaue him occasion to marry you to some prince worthy your birth and beauty.

There is no scene corresponding to this passage in the play, and Wilkins had recourse to Twine for this reason, though he added one or two details from an earlier scene of the play. Wilkins relies most obviously on Twine for material not contained in the play – in his first chapter (which describes events before the beginning of the play), in the description of the statue (barely mentioned in the play), in the description of the storm (which Gower disposes of in four lines), in the description of the wedding (not described at all), and Marina's song, absent from the text of the play as we have it. Although there are many minor borrowings from Twine, it is certain from the nature of the major borrowings that Wilkins was following the play as closely as possible, and using Twine mainly to fill in gaps.

How closely he followed the play at times can be seen from the blank-verse fossils which appear in passages of dialogue in the novel. Most of them are listed below: [1]

(*a*) As if that glorious outsides were a wall
Could keep heauens eye from knowing our intents . . .

(*b*) These prowd incestuous creatures where they sate,
Leauing their faces blasted, and their bodies
Such a contempfull obiect on the earth,
That all those eyes . . .

(*c*)               I, traytour,
That thus disguised, art stolne into my Court,
With the witchcraft of thy actions to bewitch,
The yeelding spirit of my tender Childe.

(*d*) He came into his Court in search of honour,
And not to be a rebell to his State,
His bloud was yet vntainted, but with the heate,
Got by the wrong the king had offered him,
And that he boldly durst, and did defie,
Himselfe, his subiectes, and the prowdest danger,
That eyther tyranny or treason could
Inflict vpon him.

(*e*) If euer he, by motion, or by letters,
By amorous glaunces, or by any meanes
That Louers vse to compasse their disseignes
Had sought to be a friend . . .

[1] pp. 41, 50, 51, 52, 59, 105.

(*f*) A stragling *Theseus* borne we knowe not where

(*g*) Equalles to equalls, good to good is ioyned,
    This not being so, the bauine of your minde
    In rashnesse kindled, must againe bee quenched,
    Or purchase our displeasure. And for you sir,
    First learn to know, I banish you my Court . . .

(*h*)              Poor inch of Nature
    Thou arte as rudely welcome to the worlde,
    As euer Princesse Babe was,
    And hast as chiding a natiuitie,
    As fire, ayre, earth, and water can affoord thee . . .

(*i*) But say *Lichorida*, how doth my Queene?

(*j*) I haue bin tossed from wrong to iniurie

(*k*) My mother died in paines and pangs of child-birth,
    And burial was denyed her on the earth.

It will be observed that of these eleven passages – another is discussed below[1] – containing some thirty lines of verse, there are traces of only four in the text of the play. There are several possible explanations of this phenomenon:

   1. That Wilkins dropped accidentally into blank verse and that many of the passages quoted above were not from the play.

   2. That the play originally contained many lines

[1] p. 65.

which were omitted accidentally – through bad reporting or bad printing – from the Quarto.

3. That the play was revised, but that lines were also omitted accidentally.

The first explanation can, I think, be rejected. It is quite incredible that such passages as (d) and (g) could have been written accidentally. It is true that Mr John Munro tried to show [1] that Wilkins elsewhere wrote verse by mistake; but the example he gave from *Three Miseries of Barbary* can be read as verse only by ignoring the natural accents:

> At length bowing to the earth, she fell
> At the Kings feete, and with a pretty smile
> Beganne to tell a tale of the Larke and the Crow: –
> The shutting vppe of her mortal being, –
> That the Larke was the Bird of the morning,
> And of the Day, and therefore might be bold,
> To challenge the mornings due, and all Kytes
> Of the day; But the Crow
> Was the Bird of the night and had nothing
> To do with the morning.

Of these ten lines only one can reasonably be regarded as blank verse. One has only to compare the *Pericles* novel to see that Wilkins was obviously there transprosing a play, and keeping close to the original.

We are left with the remaining two explanations. If we examine those passages of verse of which there are traces in the play, it is difficult to decide whether Wilkins

[1] *T.L.S.*, 11 October 1947.

or the Quarto gives the better text. If we turn (*d*) into direct speech it begins:

> I came into your Court in search of honour,
> And not to be a rebel to your state.

For these lines the Quarto prints: [1]

> I came into your court for honour's cause,
> And not to be a rebel to her state.

Either version is possible, though Wilkins was probably right to read *your state*. The other lines in that passage may have been omitted accidentally from the Quarto, or cut in a later performance or in process of revision. Similarly, all except the first two words of (*c*) are missing from the Quarto. They may have been cut so that Pericles could react more immediately to the word 'Traitor' with the line: [2]

> Even in his throat – unless it be the King –
> That calls me traitor I return the lie.

But these lines are so bad that we may suspect that the correct version was nearer to Wilkins:

> That were it any in his Court
> except himselfe, durst call him traytor,
> euen in his bosome he would write the lie.

A change of pronouns would make the last nine words a more vigorous line than that given in the Quarto.

To get a respectable text from (*h*) we ought probably to conflate the two versions. The Quarto reads: [3]

[1] II. v. 60–1.   [2] II. v. 55–6.   [3] III. i. 27–37.

Thou art the rudeliest welcome to this world
That ever was prince's child. Happy what follows!
Thou hast as chiding a nativity
As fire, air, water, earth, and heaven, can make
To herald thee from the womb.

The correct text should read, perhaps:

Poor inch of nature,
Thou art as rudely welcome to this world
As ever prince's babe was. Happy what follows!
Thou hast as chiding a nativity,
As fire, air, water, earth, and heaven, can make,
To herald thee from the womb.

The line 'I have bin tossed from wrong to iniurie' does not appear in the Quarto; but Pericles in a later context says:[1]

I think thou said'st
Thou hadst been toss'd from wrong to injiry.

This would seem to suggest that Marina had used these words and that they were either omitted by the reporter or omitted inadvertently by Shakespeare.

None of these passages provide definite evidence which would enable us to decide which of the explanations to accept. But there is a more extended passage of concealed blank verse in Wilkins' novel which it will be necessary to examine in detail. The following is his version of the dialogue between Marina and Lysimachus.[2] I have, where necessary, turned Wilkins' *oratio obliqua* into *oratio recta*;

[1] V. i. 129.　　　　[2] pp. 88–91.

## Shakespeare's Hand in *Pericles*

I have added a few monosyllabic words, omitted a few
words, and made two small changes. Although some
lines are still metrically imperfect, they are less so than
many lines in the Quarto text of the play; and there are
some passages – in which no alterations have been
necessary – of reasonably competent blank verse. The
first part of Marina's first speech (8–22), Lysimachus'
second speech (29–32), and the last lines of his last speech
may be given as examples.

*Lys.* I am the Governor whose authority
 Can wink at those blemishes that *you* yourself
 And that *this* sinful house could cast upon you:
 Or my displeasure punish at my pleasure;
 Which . . . thy beauty shall not privilege thee from,  5
 Nor my affection (which hath drawn me *here*) abate,
 If thou with further lingering withstand me.

*Mar.* If as you say, my lord, you are the Governor,
 Let not your authority which should teach you
 To rule others be the means to make you  10
 Mis-govern yourself. If the eminence
 Of your place came unto you by descent
 And the royalty of your blood, let not your life
 Prove your birth a bastard. If it were
 Thrown upon you by opinion, make good  15
 That opinion was the cause to make you great.
 What reason is there in your justice, who
 Have power over all, to undo any?
 If you take from me mine honour, you are like him
 That makes a gap into forbidden ground,  20
 After whom too many enter; and you are guilty
 Of all their evils. My life is yet unspotted,

My chastity unstained *even* in thought;
Then if your violence deface this building,
The workmanship of heaven, made up for good,    25
And not to be the exercise
Of sin's intemperance, you do kill your own honour,
Abuse your own justice, and impoverish me.

*Lys.*  Why! This house wherein thou livest
Is even the receptacle of all men's sins    30
And nurse of wickedness. How canst thou then
Be otherwise than naught that livest in it?

*Mar.*  It is not good, when you that are the Governor,
Who should live well, the better to be bold
To punish evil, do know that there is such a roof,    35
And yet come under it.
Is there . . . necessity, my yet good lord,
If there be fire before me that I must strait
Then thither fly and burn myself? Or if,
Suppose this house (which too too many feel    40
Such houses are) should be the doctor's patrimony
And surgeon's feeding, follows it therefore
That I must needs infect myself
To give them maintenance? O my good lord,
Kill me, but not deflower me! Punish me    45
How you please, so you spare my chastity:
And since it is all the dowry that . . . the gods
Have given and men have left to me, do not
You take it from me. Make me your servant,
I will willingly obey you; make me your bondwoman, 50
I will accompt it freedom. Let me be
The worst that is called vile, so I may still
Live honest, I am content: or if you think it . . .
Too blest a happiness to leave me so,

Let me even now, now in this minute die,                    55
And I'll accompt my death more happy than
My birth.

*Lys.*          Now surely this is Virtue's image,
Or rather Virtue's self, sent down from heaven
A while to reign on earth, to teach us *all*
What we should be. Lady, for such your virtues        60
*Show that you* are, a far more worthy style
Your beauty challenges, and no way less
Your beauty can promise me *than what* you are.
I hither came with thoughts intemperate,
Foul and deformed: the which your pains so well        65
Have laved that they are now white. Continue still
To all so. And for my part,
Who hither came but to have paid the price,
A piece of gold for your virginity,
*I* now *do* give you twenty to relieve                70
Your honesty. It shall become you still
To be even as you are, a piece of goodness
The best wrought up that ever nature made,
And if that any shall enforce you ill,
If you but send to me, I am your friend.            75

Mr Philip Edwards agrees that Wilkins was closely
following the play in this passage, but he argues that the
version given in the Quarto is a corruption of the identical
version of the scene, not a corruption of a hypothetical
revision.[1]

The elements of these two extracts (i.e. from Wilkins and
the Quarto) are not really dissimilar, though the items in the
colloquies are in a different order and though Wilkins treats

[1] *Op. cit.*, p. 43.

the whole very much more fully . . . I hold that the scene in the Quarto is not a revision but a corruption of the scene which Wilkins reports and of which he gives the true sense.

Mr Edwards proceeds to call attention to the remarkable brevity of the 'two crucial speeches' Marina addresses to Lysimachus:

After a mere sentence appealing to his honour, Lysimachus is marvelling at her *wisdom*, and after what is really only a passionate and inarticulate cry, he is marvelling at her *eloquence* – 'I did not thinke thou couldst haue spoke so well, nere dremp't thou couldst'. An affecting cry is not what the age called eloquence. What we need is amplification into really persuasive arguments – and Wilkins at the relevant points supplies just that very eloquence that is needed; we are given finely phrased, finely argued appeals which have all the power required to amaze, shame and convince Lysimachus. Moreover, these appeals carry striking verse-rhythms. Surely they must represent parts of the scene omitted in the Quarto's report.

An editor who accepted this view would presumably be bound to include in his text of the play the seventy-five lines of the Wilkins version, more or less as given above, though doubtless with some emendations in the obviously faulty lines. But it is very doubtful whether such an editorial procedure would meet with the general approval of critics, even of those who acknowledge the brilliance and persuasiveness of Mr Edwards' article.

The only passages in the Quarto which correspond verbally to the scene as given by Wilkins are the following:[1]

[1] IV. 6. 96, 99, 100, 86, 118.

(*a*) my authority shall not see thee, or
    else look friendly upon thee     (1-2)
(*b*) if you were born to honour     (11-13)
(*c*) if put upon you, make the judgement
    good, that thought you worthy of it.     (14-16)
(*d*) Do you know this house to be a
    place of such resort, and will
    come into 't.     (35-6)
(*e*) A piece of virtue, and I doubt
    not but thy training hath been noble.     (72-3)

Out of seventy-five lines the Quarto therefore succeeds in reproducing, and then only partially, the phrasing of eight or nine. This is a scene which Mr Edwards ascribes to the more accurate of the two reporters, responsible for the last three acts of the play. If one compares his competence in this scene with that displayed in Act III, Scene I, Act V, Scene I, or even Act III, Scene II, the difference is remarkable. In Act III, Scene I, although he blunders, as we have seen in ll. 30-4, he is much closer to the original than in any of the Marina–Lysimachus speeches; and though there are four errors in Pericles' first speech (e.g., *Then storme* for *Thou stormest* and *my wife* for *midwife*) and four in his later great speech (ll. 56-69 *in oare* for *in the ooze*, *ayre* for *aye*, *Taper* for *Paper* – corrected in the second edition – *Coffin* for *coffer*) these may be errors of the compositor. The speeches are obviously very close to Shakespeare's original. In Act III, Scene II (set by the same compositor) the verse is nearly all printed incorrectly, and even when it is re-arranged by editors they have, as Mr Edwards says, 'to help themselves with a plethora of short and hypermetrical lines'. Yet even in this scene

F      69

there are substantial passages which appear to reproduce accurately the words of the original in the correct order. Cerimon's speech [1] beginning 'I hold it ever' requires only a single emendation – the insertion of 'I' in l. 31. In the Wilkins version of this scene there are only two lines of verse:

> Thou hast a bodie euen drowned with woe
> Have raised impouerished bodies, like to this.

The corresponding lines in the Quarto are:

> Thou hast a heart
> That ever cracks for woe.
> Who was by good appliance recovered.

Mr Edwards argues [2] that in the second case Wilkins, who makes the Egyptians the restorers, not the restored, is more likely to reproduce what Shakespeare wrote.

In Act V, Scene I almost all the verse is printed as prose, but surely Mr Edwards exaggerates the corruption of the text when he says [3] 'we have in these later acts only the *disjecta membra* of once powerful verse'. There are, it is true, some suspicious repetitions, characteristic of a reported text, e.g.,

> I am great with woe and shall deliver weeping
> Lychorida hath oft delivered weeping.

But there are, once again, considerable stretches of what appears to be Shakespearian verse. In these three scenes, therefore, the surprising thing is not the corruption apparent in places but the accuracy achieved elsewhere,

[1] III. ii. 26 ff.     [2] *Op. cit.*, p. 41.     [3] p. 38.

and if one compares these three scenes with the Lysimachus–Marina scene one is struck forcibly by the abject failure of the hypothetical reporter to capture more than a few phrases in that scene, as well as by the curious fact that it is the only scene of which Wilkins recollects more than a few lines here and there. Mr Edwards argues [1] that the second reporter began well in the first scene of Act III:

> But his eagerness to get all right flags, and he writes down what he recalls partly in verse, partly in prose and so we lose sight, presumably for ever, of the genuine version of the last three acts, from the opening of III, ii.

This seems to imply that the reporter did not use shorthand – and no existing system of shorthand [2] would have enabled him to achieve the accuracy of the opening scene of Act III – but that he relied on his memory, presumably after a number of visits to the playhouse. I do not think that this explains the extraordinary failure with the Marina–Lysimachus scene. When a reported text varies greatly in accuracy from scene to scene – e.g., the bad Quarto of *Hamlet* – it can be explained by the fact that the pirate was a small-part actor who could report accurately the scenes in which he himself appeared.[3] But it is difficult to explain *Pericles* in such a way. Neither Marina nor Lysimachus could have been the pirates because of the hopeless text of the scene they have together. Lychorida

[1] p. 38.
[2] See G. I. Duthie, *Elizabethan Shorthand and the First Quarto of King Lear* (1949).
[3] See, e.g., G. I. Duthie, *The Bad Quarto of Hamlet*.

could not have been the pirate because she does not appear in the later scenes. Pericles can be ruled out both because Burbage was above suspicion and because he does not appear in Act III, Scene III. It appears, therefore, to be impossible to explain the text by the assumption that one of the actors was the pirate.

If therefore we fall back on the theory that the second reporter by visiting the theatre many times contrived to reproduce some speeches with astonishing accuracy – even down to the correct line-division and necessary abbreviations – but that he became less conscientious later on, we are still without an explanation of the vast superiority of his reporting of Act V, Scene I to that of the brothel-scene. One could understand him getting tired and inaccurate as the play progressed, but not that he should suddenly improve; and, in any case, after repeated visits to the playhouse one would not expect any great difference in the accuracy of his reporting of different scenes.

If we now turn again to the Lysimachus–Marina dialogue as reported by Wilkins, we cannot but observe that although the verse is reasonably competent, it is quite different in kind from the verse preserved either in Act III, Scene I or Act V, Scene I. The latter could have been written only in Shakespeare's final period. The former could not possibly have been written as late as 1607 and, it is fairly safe to say, is quite unlikely to have been written by him at any stage of his career. This difference of style is so apparent that one is driven to assume that the brothel-scene belongs to an earlier stratum of the play, and that, when one makes all allowances for the bad text of the Quarto, it attempts to reproduce a later version of the scene.

If this argument is sound, and at least one scene in the play underwent revision between the time when Wilkins saw it and the publication of the Quarto, is it not probable that the same thing is true of other scenes? The difference between the first two acts and the last three from the point of view of style may be due, at least in part, to the fact that Shakespeare made fewer changes in the first two acts of the play. This would also account for the greater number of verbal parallels in the chapters of Wilkins corresponding to the first two acts.

The strong case made by Mr Edwards for the existence of two reporters would be somewhat weakened if we could be reasonably certain that the novel and the Quarto are based on two different versions of the play, for if the early acts were written in a more primitive verse than the later acts – with more regular lines, often end-stopped, and with a fair amount of rhyme – it would not be surprising if the compositor found it easier to preserve the lines. It will be recalled that Mercutio's Queen Mab speech and several of the Nurse's speeches in *Romeo and Juliet* were originally printed as prose, and that Shakespeare did not begin every line with a capital letter.[1]

We need not necessarily reject Mr Edwards' view that two reporters were concerned with the preparation of the Quarto text. But whether there were two reporters or one, we are driven back to an earlier hypothesis – that an unknown dramatist wrote a play on the Apollonius story some months or years before the publication of Wilkins'

[1] On the evidence of *Sir Thomas More*.

version. This play was revised by Shakespeare *c.* 1607, cursorily in the first two acts, extensively in the remaining three. He altered the names of the leading characters. Wilkins, who was familiar with the old *Pericles*, wrote his novel – or at any rate finished it – after Shakespeare's revision of the play had been performed, for he uses the Shakespearian names for his characters and perhaps made a few changes to bring his tale nearer to the revised version of the play. One might explain his almost verbatim rendering of the Lysimachus scene by suggesting that Wilkins, who wrote for Shakespeare's company, obtained the original sheets of this scene when they were superseded by Shakespeare's version. This is, of course, pure speculation; but it is difficult to explain, without some such hypothesis, the fact that this is the only chapter of the novel containing many blank-verse fossils.

Soon afterwards Gosson obtained a reported text of the revised play, and there is one piece of evidence to suggest that the pirates made some slight use of Wilkins. Pericles' lines in Act II, Scene III –

> A Gentleman of *Tyre*, my name *Pericles*,
> My education beene in Artes and Armes:
> Who looking for aduentures in the world –

correspond exactly, even to spelling and capitalization, to the passage given by Wilkins.[1]

hee was a Gentleman of *Tyre*, his name *Pericles*, his education been in Artes and Armes, who looking for aduentures in the world . . .

[1] p. 40.

## Shakespeare's Hand in *Pericles*

It looks as though the verse of the Quarto has been clumsily adapted from the *oratio obliqua* of the novel. Mr Edwards, who inclines to the view that Shakespeare wrote the whole play, and that Wilkins and the Quarto provide reports of the play as written by Shakespeare, would have to bring himself to believe that where the reports are identical they reproduce accurately what Shakespeare actually wrote.[1] But in my opinion not only is it incredible that Shakespeare wrote the lines but it is also unlikely that any dramatist would have written them in that form.

This hypothesis which seeks to account for the facts is somewhat complex, but so are the facts it seeks to explain. It does, I think, account for all the facts, which neat and simple hypotheses signally fail to do. I have deliberately avoided any discussion of the authorship of the Ur-*Pericles*. It is hardly possible now to suppose that Wilkins was the author of it, as he would not in that case have given such a poor report of it in his novel. Mr H. D. Gray argued [2] that the play was similar to Heywood's *Fortune by Land and Sea* and *The Fair Maid of the West*; that Heywood was fond of the chorus and the dumb show; that he has plays on the preservation of the innocence of girls brought up in a tavern or a brothel; and that the Captain in *The Royall King and a Loyall Subject*, like Lysimachus, protests that he did not come to corrupt the inmate of a brothel. Mr Gray convinced himself that the style of the first two acts of *Pericles* is not unlike Heywood's. I have

[1] Unless, I suppose, the text of the play was influenced by the text of the novel, or vice versa.
[2] *P.M.L.A.* XL, pp. 507–29.

suggested elsewhere [1] that the evidence put forward by Mr H. D. Sykes that Wilkins wrote the play might be considered in relation to the evidence that Heywood wrote it. The two dramatists are thought to have collaborated in the play from which *The Miseries of Inforst Mariage* and *The Yorkshire Tragedy* were derived, and they might conceivably have collaborated in the Ur-*Pericles*. This might, perhaps, account for Wilkins' close familiarity with some scenes and his comparative ignorance of others. But the evidence is clearly inconclusive. When one is dealing with a bad Quarto one must expect to find the text contaminated with echoes from other plays, and the parallels with Heywood's work, with Wilkins' *Miseries of Inforst Mariage*, and with *Law Tricks* may throw no real light on the authorship of the Ur-*Pericles*.

[1] *Op. cit.*, p. xi.

# V

## *Pericles*

Whether we accept Mr Philip Edwards' view that the difference between the first two acts of the play and the remainder is due to the differing skill of two reporters, or assume that Shakespeare based his play on the work of another dramatist, making few alterations in the opening acts and completely rewriting the last three, we may agree that the text given in the Quarto is a bad one, and almost certainly reported. But the two theories have different editorial implications. Those who believe that Wilkins' novel is based on an earlier play which Shakespeare revised should be less ready to accept readings from the novel into the text of the last three acts of the play than those who regard Wilkins' novel as a kind of rival report. On the other hand, those who think that Wilkins was reporting Shakespeare's play ought to have the courage of their convictions and print the Lysimachus–Marina dialogue almost as given in the novel. In any case we may assume that the text of the play is so poor that it is only a garbled version of what Shakespeare actually wrote. Whole lines and parts of lines have been omitted by reporters or compositors, and others have been so corrupted that not even the most confident textual critic can hope to restore them. On the other hand, there are speeches, and even whole scenes, where little emendation is required, and which appear to be so accurate that Hardin Craig could believe that they must have been printed from Shakespeare's foul papers.

Although, as I have argued, Shakespeare was probably using an old play as his main source, it was his usual custom to consult more than one source.[1] Wilkins made extensive use of Twine's version of the Apollonius story in *The Painfull Adventures of Pericles*, and it is not unlikely that Shakespeare made use of it too. It was readily accessible in the 1607 reprint, but it is impossible to prove that Shakespeare consulted it. He would certainly have referred to Gower's *Confessio Amantis*. It is probable that Shakespeare himself was responsible for the re-naming of the main characters; and, as I have suggested elsewhere,[2] he may have taken Marina from the story of the Mexican girl who became interpreter to Cortes and who was baptized under that name. She had been born the daughter of a chief, and on her father's death she had been sold to some Indians by her own mother, so as to ensure the succession of her son by her second husband. Years later, while acting as interpreter to Cortes in the province in which she was born, she was seen and recognized by her mother and half-brother, who were terrified that she would take vengeance on them. But Marina, either moved by their tears or taking her newly acquired religion seriously, forgave them and made them presents. This story of a princess, who was sold into slavery by her mother and step-father and who forgave her mother

[1] Cf. K. Muir, *Shakespeare's Sources* (1957), *passim*.
[2] *English Studies*, XXXIX (1958), pp. 74–5.

and the son for whom the crime had been committed
when she had them in her power, would have appealed
to Shakespeare while he was writing the plays of the last
period. The story resembles the plot of *The Tempest* in
one respect, and the plot of *Pericles* in others. Unfor-
tunately the full story is not known to have been published in Shakespeare's lifetime. The brief version given
by Francisco Lopez de Gomara (whose *Historie of the
Conquest of the Weast India, now called new Spayne* appeared
in translation in 1578) lacks the touch of maternal
treachery and the sequel of filial forgiveness. The stealing
of the child, her name, and her gift of the tongues would
be somewhat tenuous links with *Pericles*; but Shakespeare
may have come across a published version of the story
nearer to the one outlined above, and have been reminded
of the Mexican Marina when he read of Dionyza's treatment of Apollonius' daughter, of the seizure of the girl
by pirates, and of her escape from the brothel by means
of her various accomplishments, as Marina earned a
Spanish husband by her gift of the tongues. The name
Marina, moreover, would strike Shakespeare as appropriate for one who was born at sea.

Ben Jonson referred to *Pericles*, in a moment of pique,
as 'a mouldy tale' – a hit, presumably, not merely at the
antiquity of the Apollonius story, but at its naïvety. It
consists of a series of events linked together only by the
fact that they illustrate the operations of fortune in the
life of the hero. There is no integral connexion between
Apollonius' wooing of the daughter of Antiochus and
the later episodes of his marriage, the loss of his wife and
daughter, and his final reunion with them. Apollonius

happens to meet his bride when he leaves Tyre for fear of the wrath of Antiochus. Even if Shakespeare had dramatized only the second part of the story – the separation of his hero from his wife and daughter and his ultimate reunion with them – he would not have been able to imbue it with the kind of significance to be found in *Cymbeline* or *The Winter's Tale*. Posthumus loses his wife, and Leontes his wife and children, through their own fault; and they earn the restoration of their lost ones by their penitence. The misfortunes which befall Pericles can hardly be said to be due to his own sins, though it has been suggested that he was paying for his inability to recognize until too late the evil hidden beneath the fair exterior of Antiochus' daughter. It is possible, however, that an attempt by Shakespeare to impose significance on his material has been blurred by the corruption of the text.[1] In Act II, Scene IV Simonides informs Thaisa's suitors that she will not marry for at least twelve months:

> One twelve moons more she'll wear Diana's livery.
> This by the eye of Cynthia hath she vow'd,
> And on her virgin honour will not break it.

We are not told definitely whether Simonides is speaking the truth. His words immediately after the departure of the suitors – 'So, they are well despatch'd' – suggest, perhaps, that he has invented the vow to rid himself of the suitors so as to leave the field free for the favoured Pericles. Whether the vow was an invention or not, it is worth noting that Diana is mentioned several times in the Shakespearian parts of the play and once, as Lucina, in the

[1] Cf. *N.Q.* (1948), p. 362.

first scene. (Lucina, incidentally, was Twine's name for
Thaisa.) Pericles prays to Lucina during his wife's
labour –

> Divinest patroness, and midwife gentle
> To those that cry by night –

and his prayer is rejected. When Thaisa is restored to life,
her first words are addressed to the same goddess – 'O
dear Diana!' Assuming that she will never see Pericles
again – why is not explained – she decides to put on a
vestal livery and serve as priestess in the temple of Diana
at Ephesus. Gower, as chorus, speaks of Diana as
Marina's mistress. Pericles vows 'by bright Diana' to
leave his hair 'unscissored'. Marina, appropriately, prays
to Diana in the brothel; and in the last act Diana appears
to Pericles in a vision, telling him to visit her temple at
Ephesus. He promises to obey 'Celestial Dian, goddess
argentine'. The last scene takes place in the temple. In his
address to the goddess, Pericles describes his child as
wearing yet Diana's 'silver livery'; and, after his wife has
been restored to him, he declares:

> Pure Dian, bless thee for thy vision! I
> Will offer night-oblations to thee.

It looks as though Shakespeare intended Thaisa's time in
the temple to be a means of expiating the sin of taking the
name of the goddess in vain, and that his intentions have
been partially hidden by the corrupt text.[1] But the trials
which Pericles and his family undergo are also a means of

---

[1] To judge from the Wilkins novel, Shakespeare did not find the
broken vow motivation in the source-play.

testing them; and their final reunion is in accordance with Jupiter's pronouncement in *Cymbeline* –

> Whom best I love I cross; to make my gift
> The more delay'd, delighted –

an echo, no doubt, of the scriptural 'Whom the Lord loveth, He chasteneth'.

It has often been observed that in the plays of the final period the characters are much less complex, less realistic, than they had been in the great tragedies and comedies of Shakespeare's middle period. They are not merely simplified: they tend to be puppets, unable to control their own destinies. Although Hamlet speaks of the 'divinity that shapes our ends', Malvolio declares that 'all is fortune', Kent exclaims that 'it is the stars that govern our condition', Edmund acknowledges that 'the wheel has come full circle', Macbeth comes to think that life is 'a tale told by an idiot', and Othello asks despairingly 'Who can control his fate?', we recognize in all those plays that fate works through character. In *Cymbeline* and *The Winter's Tale*, although human evil and weakness are equally apparent, these do not produce their logical results, since the action of the play appears to be controlled by the gods.[1] Mr T. S. Eliot has suggested that Shakespeare in his last plays makes us feel not so much that his characters are creatures like ourselves, as that we are creatures like his characters, 'taking part like them in no common action of which we are for the most part

[1] The following paragraphs are based on a lecture given at Wayne State University, Detroit, to be published in a volume entitled *Last Periods*.

unaware'. The characters are 'the work of a writer who has finally seen through the dramatic action of men into a spiritual action which transcends it'. A similar idea is expressed in the well-known lines in *Murder in the Cathedral*:

> Neither does the actor suffer
> Nor the patient act. But both are fixed
> In an eternal action, an eternal patience
> To which all must consent that it may be willed
> And which all must suffer that they may will it
> That the pattern may subsist, for the pattern is the action
> And the suffering, that the wheel may turn and still
> Be forever still.

But although Shakespeare might see some such pattern in the story of Apollonius – the converting of the wheel of fortune into the wheel of Providence – the difficulty remained of imposing a strictly dramatic unity on such an episodic story. Shakespeare had read Sidney's amusing account of a dramatic treatment of this kind of material:

> You shall have *Asia* of the one side, and *Affricke* of the other, and so manie other under Kingdomes, that the Player when he comes in, must ever begin with telling where he is, or else the tale will not be conceived. Now you shall have three Ladies walke to gather flowers, and then we must beleeve the stage to be a garden. By and by we heare newes of shipwreck in the same place, then we are to blame if we accept it not for a Rock. Upon the back of that, comes out a hidious monster with fire and smoke, and then the miserable beholders are bound to take it for a Cave: while in the meane time two Armies flie in, represented with foure swords & bucklers, and then what hard hart wil not receive it for a pitched field. Now of time, they are much more

liberall. For ordinarie it is, that two yoong Princes fall in love, after many traverses she is got with child, delivered of a faire boy: he is lost, groweth a man, falleth in love, and is readie to get an other childe, and all this in two houres space: which howe absurd it is in sence, even sence may imagine: and Arte hath taught, and all auncient examples justified . . . But they will say, how then shall we set foorth a storie, which contains both many places and many times?

Sidney answers that a tragedy is not tied to the laws of history, that events can be reported by a *Nuntius*, and that

if they will represent an Historie, they must not (as *Horace* saith) beginne *ab ovo*, but they must come to the principall poynte of that one action which they will represent.

In the choruses of *Henry V* Shakespeare seems to be apologizing for not taking Sidney's advice; and Father Time, in *The Winter's Tale*, asks the audience to impute it not a crime that he disobeys the unity of time and slides over sixteen years. In *Pericles* Shakespeare uses the device of Ancient Gower, whether borrowed from an earlier play or suggested to Shakespeare by his reading of *Confessio Amantis*. Although the Gower choruses would not satisfy a modern student of Middle English, they do suggest, with remarkable skill, the general atmosphere of Gower's garrulous masterpiece. His rudimentary art, with its monotonous octosyllabic lines, its neutral diction, its rare imagery, and its pervasive moralizing, appealed to the simple curiosity of its readers. They asked, 'What happened next?' The causal relationship between one incident and the next and the psychology of the characters were equally unimportant. Incident followed after incident, with a running commentary designed to point the appropriate morals. Shakespeare has caught the manner to perfection, even though he cannot refrain from an occasional touch of better poetry. He doubtless recalled Chaucer's epithet for Gower – 'moral' – when he penned the last lines of the play:

> In Antiochus and his daughter you have heard
> Of monstrous lust the due and just reward:
> In Pericles, his queen, and daughter, seen,
> Although assail'd with fortune fierce and keen,
> Virtue preserv'd from fell destruction's blast,
> Led on by heaven, and crown'd with joy at last.
> In Helicanus may you well descry
> A figure of truth, of faith, of loyalty;
> In reverend Cerimon there well appears
> The worth that learned charity aye wears . . .

The naïvety of Gower's chorus provides a suitable framework for the play. Shakespeare was asking his audience to listen to the story in an unsophisticated frame of mind, forgetting for the time being the kind of intelligent response they would make to *King Lear* or *Twelfth Night*, and adopting rather the simpler and relaxed attitude suitable to a play like *Mucedorus* or *The Rare Triumphs of Love and Fortune*. It is said that the tale of Apollonius is still told by professional story-tellers in the villages and round camp-fires in the Lebanon. A good thing, we are told, is the better for being ancient:

*Et bonum quo antiquius, eo melius.*

It was presumably because he wished to suggest the unsophicated way in which the story should be received that

the producer of *Pericles* at the Memorial Theatre, Stratford-upon-Avon, in 1958, hit upon the ingenious idea of
turning a Middle English poet, Gower, into a Negro
boatswain, and provided him with an audience on the
stage of simple-minded seamen who followed the story
with open-eyed wonder. But it should, of course, be
borne in mind that when a sophisticated audience is asked
to respond in an unsophisticated way it does so with some
ambivalence. When Mr Eliot, for example, introduces
into *Murder in the Cathedral* verse apparently imitated
from *Everyman*, the effect on an audience is complex. It
does not react in a purely unsophisticated way, but with
a mixture of simplicity and sophistication.

When all allowances have been made for textual corruption, it is apparent that both character and incident in
*Pericles* have been deliberately simplified. The characters
are either very good or very evil. The daughter of
Antiochus in the first act, though surpassingly beautiful,

> clothed like a bride
> For the embracements even of Jove himself,

is entirely evil. The mouldering remains of her former
suitors which tell Pericles

> with speechless tongues and semblance pale,
> That without covering, save yon field of stars,
> Here they stand martyrs, slain in Cupid's wars;
> And with dead cheeks advise thee to desist
> From going on death's net,

inform the audience that they are watching a romantic and
unrealistic play, set in a remote and unreal world. It is a
world where murderers carry out their orders with the

minimum of fuss, as when Antiochus orders the assassination of Pericles:

> Thaliard, behold here's poison and here's gold;
> We hate the Prince of Tyre, and thou must kill him.
> It fits thee not to ask the reason why,
> Because we bid it. Say, is it done?

Thaliard replies laconically: 'My lord, 'tis done.' Even in the Shakespearian part of the play, where 'Leonine, a murderer' is endowed with some scruples, these are felt to be a tribute to Marina's beauty and goodness rather than a means of humanizing Leonine:

> I will do't; but yet she is a goodly creature.

The scene between Cleon and Dionyza is almost a parody of scenes between Albany and Goneril or between Macbeth and his wife. Dionyza, like the hypocritical and devilish Queen in *Cymbeline*, has no redeeming characteristics: she is a picturesque and melodramatic villain.

On the other side of the moral fence, the good people are perfectly good – Helicanus is a perfect counsellor, Marina is a paragon, Cerimon is a type of aristocratic learning, benevolence, and wisdom. Only with Lysimachus is there any doubt. He has to be fundamentally decent to enable him to marry Marina; but he has to be something of a rake to enable him to be a prospective client in the brothel. Most of Shakespeare's audience would not have worried about this; and they would cheerfully assume that he had been converted, as even Boult is converted, by Marina's purity. But Shakespeare himself seems to have had a twinge of uneasiness on the matter, and he throws in a hint at the end of the brothel-scene that Lysimachus, like Duke Vincentio in *Measure for Measure* or a modern social scientist, was making a study of the red-light district for reputable motives:

> Had I brought hither a corrupted mind
> Thy speech had altered it . . .
> For me, be you thoughten
> That I came with no ill intent; for to me
> The very doors and windows savour vilely.

These lines are difficult to reconcile with the way Lysimachus is greeted by the Bawd as an old customer, and we have to assume either that Lysimachus is whitewashing himself to Marina or that Shakespeare belatedly realized that Lysimachus as he had depicted him was not a suitable husband for her.[1]

There are no lines in the first two acts which are certainly Shakespeare's, though there are a number which could be his. It is a thrilling moment in the theatre when at the beginning of Act III the voice of Shakespeare is heard, indubitable and potent, with a tempest at sea to match the storm in *King Lear*:

> Thou god of this great vast, rebuke these surges,
> Which wash both heaven and hell; and thou that hast
> Upon the winds command, bind them in brass,

[1] The verse in Lysimachus' speech is so bad that we may suppose that the text is corrupt. In Wilkins' novel, as we have seen, Lysimachus says 'and for my parte, who hither came but to haue payd the price, a peece of gold for your virginitie'. Possibly this more nearly represents the correct text – it is, it will be noticed, in verse – but it is surely more likely that Shakespeare altered his source at this point with the object of presenting Marina a more presentable husband.

88

Having call'd them from the deep! O, still
Thy deaf'ning dreadful thunders; gently quench
Thy nimble sulphurous flashes! – O, how, Lychorida,
How does my queen? – Thou stormest venomously:
Wilt thou spit all thyself? The seaman's whistle
Is as a whisper in the ears of death,
Unheard.

The whole scene is palpably Shakespearian, and this is
evident in spite of the misprints, the mislineations, and
one obvious omission in the Quarto. On the whole, the
reporter has done his work surprisingly well, better than
one could expect from existing methods of shorthand.[1] A
later speech in the same scene exhibits both the colloquial
ease and the magical phrasing of Shakespeare's last
period:

A terrible childbed hast thou had, my dear;
No light, no fire. Th'unfriendly elements
Forgot thee utterly; nor have I time
To give thee hallow'd to thy grave, but straight
Must cast thee scarcely coffin'd, in the ooze;
Where, for a monument upon thy bones,
And aye-remaining lamps the belching whale
And humming water must o'erwhelm thy corpse,
Lying with simple shells.

[1] In the above speech the Quarto prints *The god* for *Thou god, then
storme* for *Thou stormest*, and *Unheard* is attached not to *whisper* but to
the word *Lichorida* which follows. These errors might well be due
to the compositor rather than to the reporter. Although we have no
good text with which to compare that of the *Pericles* quarto, it
would appear to be far more accurate in this scene than (say) the bad
quarto of *Hamlet*.

## Shakespeare as Collaborator

This is not the first storm in the play, and the recurrence of tempest imagery even in the early acts made Wilson Knight suspect that Shakespeare was revising an early play of his own. At the beginning of Act II Pericles had been wrecked on the shore of Pentapolis, the sole survivor; and his speech may derive any Shakespearian quality it may be thought to possess from the acquaintance of its author with Shakespeare's earlier plays:

> Yet cease your ire, you angry stars of heaven!
> Wind, rain and thunder, remember earthly man
> Is but a substance that must yield to you;
> And I, as fits my nature, do obey you.
> Alas, the sea hath cast me on the rocks,
> Wash'd me from shore to shore, and left me breath
> Nothing to think on but ensuing death.

The opening lines of this speech are reasonably effective; but the last three are a sad anti-climax, whether due to the inefficiency of the reporter or to the uncertain mastery of the author. In itself the speech can hardly be regarded as a proof that Shakespeare was himself the author of the original *Pericles*. Some account of a storm was demanded by the story at this point in the play, and any author would have had to provide it.

The scene in which Thaisa is restored, though reported less accurately than the scene in Marina's birth, is equally authentic in its conception. Cerimon, of whom Pericles later remarks –

> The Gods can have no mortal officer
> More like a god than you –

is a character of wisdom and nobility, who seems to embody the essential spirit of the plays of Shakespeare's last period. In some ways he resembles Prospero, though he lacks the touch of asperity and disillusionment of that character. He speaks in verse which is worlds away from the crudity of that used in the first two acts of the play:

> I held it ever,
> Virtue and cunning were endowments greater
> Than nobleness and riches: careless heirs
> May the two latter darken and expend,
> But immortality attends the former,
> Making a man a god. 'Tis known, I ever
> Have studied physic, through which secret art,
> By turning o'er authorities, I have,
> Together with my practice, made familiar
> To me and to my aid the blest infusions
> That dwell in vegetives, in metals, stones;
> And I can speak of the disturbances
> That nature works, and of her cures; which doth give me
> A more content in course of true delight
> Than to be thirsty after tottering honour,
> Or tie my treasure up in silken bags,
> To please the fool and death.

This self-portrait prepares the way for the 'resurrection' of Thaisa, which is accompanied by music, as Lear's had been and as Hermione's was to be. Thaisa bequeaths to death her dumbness, and Cerimon uses the jewel imagery which is taken up and developed in the last act of the play:

Behold,
Her eyelids, cases to those heavenly jewels
Which Pericles hath lost, begin to part
Their fringes of bright gold; the diamonds
Of a most praised water do appear,
To make the world twice rich.

So Cerimon, in the last scene, tells Pericles:

I op'd the coffin,
Found there rich jewels;

and Pericles is reminded of Thaisa when he sees his daughter in the ship:

Her eyes as jewel-like
And cased as richly.

This imagery is appropriate to a play which is concerned with the finding of that which was lost, and we may suspect that it was suggested, like the pearl and the chrysolite in *Othello*, by the Gospel parable of the pearl of great price.

The first of the Marina scenes (IV. 1) contains a flower passage comparable to similar ones in *The Winter's Tale*, *Cymbeline*, and *The Two Noble Kinsmen*, a superb example of tempest imagery –

Ay me! poor maid,
Born in a tempest, when my mother died,
This world to me is like a lasting storm,
Whirring me from my friends –

and one or two passages which well suggest Marina's crystalline innocence; but there are other passages of stumbling verse which appear to be corrupt. The feebleness of the following lines and the awkward internal

rhyme are presumably the ruins of a genuine Shakespearian speech:

> My father, as nurse says, did never fear,
> But cried 'Good seamen' to the sailors, galling
> His kingly hands hauling ropes,
> And clasping to the mast, endured a sea
> That almost burst the deck.

The prose of the brothel scenes is sometimes masterly
(e.g. in IV. ii.) but, as we have seen, the verse of Act IV,
Scene VI is fragmentary, and less sustained than the verse-
fossils contained in Wilkins' novel. It is not till the first
scene of Act V, in which Pericles is reunited to his
daughter, that Shakespeare's imagination seems to be
again working at full pressure, unless the weakness of the
Marina–Lysimachus scene is due to the failure of the
reporters rather than to that of the poet.

In the restoration scene,[1] tempest imagery is again used,
but now no longer expressing hatred and discord –

> Lest this great sea of joys rushing upon me
> O'erbear the shores of my mortality,
> And drown me with their sweetness.

Once again, as in *King Lear*, the restoration is accompanied by music, first by Marina's lost song, and then by
the music of the spheres; it is followed by Pericles' demand for fresh garments and by the appearance of Diana
in a vision – the first theophany in Shakespeare's works.[2]

[1] The reader may be referred to the chapter in Derek Traversi's
*Shakespeare's Last Period* and to the masterly analysis by G. Wilson
Knight in *The Crown of Life*.
[2] The appearance of Hymen in *As You Like It* is in a masque performed by human actors.

## Shakespeare as Collaborator

The quality of the scene may be illustrated by a single image.[1] In *Twelfth Night* Viola speaks of the love-sick maid who

> sat like Patience on a monument,
> Smiling at grief.

A similar image is used in this scene in *Pericles* with even greater dramatic force. The hero, meeting his daughter after many years of suffering, sees in her face the signs of her suffering and of ordeals bravely borne. He then uses the following image:

> Yet thou dost look
> Like Patience, gazing on Kings' graves, and smiling
> Extremity out of act.

This wonderful image suggests all that Marina has undergone and all that Pericles himself has endured. It suggests that Marina is a king's daughter; it suggests her courage and patience in adversity – pursued by a murderer, captured by pirates, and sold to a brothel. Pericles is to be reborn; Thaisa is to be restored to him from the sea; and the whole family is to be re-united in an earthly resurrection. This is the situation in the play, and the image is exquisitely appropriate to it. The theme of the play is the restoration of the lost and the conquest of death by love – in so far as the theme of one of Shakespeare's plays can be expressed in abstract terms. This theme, this particular scene, its antecedents and its sequel, and the face of the girl imagined by the poet called up the inevitable image

[1] This paragraph is based on a passage in my article 'The Future of Shakespeare' (*Penguin New Writing* 28).

which is not merely a symbolic description of Marina but also helps to create the vision of the play.

Journeys that end in lovers' meeting, scenes in which brother and sister, husband and wife, or parents and children meet again after long separation, when each believed the other dead, were frequent episodes in Elizabethan fiction - and in the Greek Romances on which they were sometimes based – and they have always been effective on the stage, whether in Greek tragedy or Latin comedy. Two of Euripides' most effective scenes are the meeting of Iphigenia and Orestes in Tauris and the restoration of Alcestis to her husband. Even the reunion of Egeon and his wife in *The Comedy of Errors* is a moving scene in a play which is largely farcical; the silent reunion of Isabella and Claudio is a little-recognized master-stroke in *Measure for Measure*; and the meeting of Viola and Sebastian in *Twelfth Night* is a touching climax to that play. The meeting of Pericles and Marina surpasses all these. Its effectiveness, and the effectiveness of the whole play, is due partly to Shakespeare's creation of a kind of myth which he could set up against the changes and chances of this mortal life. He is calling in a new world to redress the balance of the old, a new world in which the designs of evil men are frustrated and in which everything comes right in the end – the beautiful queen is not really dead, the beautiful princess is saved from murder and rape and the contamination of the brothel, and the hero, after more trials and tribulations than are normally the lot of man, is rewarded with unforeseen and unimagined happiness. Shakespeare is aware that his story is too good to be true, but such fables are a criticism of life as it is, and (as some think) a statement of faith. In a pagan setting he creates what is virtually an immortality myth.

The misfortunes that befall Pericles are undeserved, and the restoration to him of his wife and child is due to the inscrutable workings of Providence. In the plays which followed Shakespeare set out to eliminate accident, and to infuse the restoration theme with ethical meaning. This could be done only by replacing the workings of an arbitrary providence by the operations of sin and forgiveness. Leontes' jealousy causes the death of Mamillius, and apparently of Hermione also, the loss of Perdita, and estrangement from Polixenes. But the two kings are reconciled through the marriage of their children; and when Leontes by his penitence has earned forgiveness, Hermione is restored to him. In *Pericles* Shakespeare had dealt at length with the finding of the lost daughter and only cursorily with the reunion of husband and wife. In *The Winter's Tale* the emphasis is reversed. The father–daughter recognition takes place off stage, and Shakespeare concentrates on the reunion of Leontes and Hermione – because Leontes has sinned chiefly against her and needs her forgiveness before the play can end in reconciliation. In *Cymbeline* Imogen forgives Posthumus for his attempted murder, and their reconciliation does not require a marriage of children to cement it. In *The Tempest* Shakespeare concentrates on the act of forgiveness itself. In *The Winter's Tale* and *Cymbeline* the hero is the sinner; in *The Tempest* the hero is sinned against, and the betrayal had taken place sixteen years before. By this means Shakespeare eliminated the break of sixteen years which occurs in both *Pericles* and *The Winter's Tale*. The advantages are not all on one side; and the French critic who remarked that Shakespeare finally succeeded in obeying the unity of time by eliminating action altogether was not without some justification. The looser structure of *The Winter's Tale* is necessary to the particular effects at which Shakespeare was aiming; and the yet looser structure of *Pericles* is the only way by which the story of Apollonius could be put on the stage.

In recent years there has been a revival of interest in the play, heralded by T. S. Eliot's exquisite *Marina* and by Wilson Knight's eloquent reassessment in *The Crown of Life*, and exemplified by productions at the Old Vic and Birmingham and by two at Stratford. One Stratford production omitted the first act, and the liberties taken in the other seemed to indicate a lack of confidence in the play's ability to appeal to a modern audience. But at Birmingham the audience was captivated throughout the performance; and this was yet another indication that Shakespeare knew better than his critics, and better even than modish producers, that he had hit on precisely the right form for the material he was dramatizing, and that we have no right to deplore the taste of the groundlings who were enthusiastic when the play was first performed.

# VI

# Shakespeare's Hand in
## *The Two Noble Kinsmen*

The authorship of *The Two Noble Kinsmen* is still a matter of controversy. The plain ascription on the title-page to Shakespeare and Fletcher has been supported by the opinions of Pope, Lamb, Coleridge, De Quincey, Tennyson, Swinburne, Bradley, Masefield, E. K. Chambers, and Theodore Spencer; but Shelley, Sykes, and others have denied that Shakespeare had a hand in the play, and most modern editions exclude it, even though they include a scene or more from *Sir Thomas More* for which there is no external evidence of Shakespeare's authorship – as there is with *The Two Noble Kinsmen*. It is the aim of this chapter to prove that Shakespeare wrote part of the play.

Littledale, in what is still the best edition, made two preliminary assumptions: (1) that two authors are discernible in the play; (2) that Fletcher is one of them. Every modern critic would, no doubt, make the same assumptions. The difference of style in the two portions is apparent even to the casual reader; and general impressions are substantiated by more objective tests. Littledale, for example, applied four metrical tests to the scenes he supposed to be by two different dramatists, and arrived at the following conclusions:

|  | Fletcher | Non-Fletcher |
|---|---|---|
| Light Endings | 3 | 52 |
| Weak Endings | 1 | 35 |
| Light + Weak | 4 | 87 |
| % feminine endings | 52·9 | 28·6 |
| % unstopt lines | 24·6 | 56·1 |

The above table alone would seem to indicate that the play was written by more than one dramatist. The following table (based on that of Chambers) shows that the figures for the non-Fletcherian parts of *The Two Noble Kinsmen* correspond roughly to the figures of Shakespeare's last plays. (Chambers's figures differ slightly from

| Play | % of Feminine Endings | Light Endings | Weak Endings | Light + Weak | As % of blank verse |
|---|---|---|---|---|---|
| *Cymbeline* | 32 | 78 | 52 | 130 | 4·9 |
| *Winter's Tale* | 33 | 57 | 43 | 100 | 4·7 |
| *Tempest* | 32 | 42 | 25 | 67 | 4·5 |
| *Henry VIII* Shakespeare's part Fletcher's part | 47 32 59 | 52 45 7 | 38 37 1 | 90 82 8 | 3·4 7·1 0·5 |
| *Two Noble Kinsmen* | 30 | 50 | 34 | 84 | 8·0 |

Littledale's because there is a doubt about the authorship of one or two scenes.) These figures would clearly fit in with the theory that the non-Fletcherian scenes were written by Shakespeare. It will be observed that the percentage of feminine endings remains approximately the same (30–3), much less than the Fletcher percentage, but that the percentage of light and weak endings rises after *The Tempest*. It will likewise be observed that the percentage of feminine endings in the scenes ascribed to Fletcher in *Henry VIII* is close to the percentage in the corresponding scenes of *The Two Noble Kinsmen*. This metrical argument therefore partly depends on the assumption that *Henry VIII* was written by Shakespeare and Fletcher, though even if Shakespeare wrote the whole play the argument from light and weak endings would still be valid.

Metrical tests are no longer fashionable – it has become fashionable rather to sneer at them. This is doubtless due to the extravagant use made of them by some scholars. It would be absurd to argue that *The Tempest* was followed by *The Winter's Tale* and *Cymbeline* because of the percentages given above – 4·5, 4·7, 4·9. But it would be equally absurd to pretend that there is no significance in the complete absence of light and weak endings in Shakespeare's early plays or in their frequency after 1608. Metrical tests, after all, merely express mathematically what every competent reader will recognize instinctively – that Shakespeare's later verse is very different from his earlier verse and that, whether Shakespeare wrote them or not, there are scenes in *The Two Noble Kinsmen* which from a metrical point of view might well be his, assuming he wrote a play soon after *The Tempest*. This evidence is supported by Bradley's demonstration [1] that six or seven of the nine non-Fletcherian blank-verse scenes end with a part-line, and that this, frequent in the later plays of Shakespeare, was comparatively rare in the plays of Fletcher and Massinger.

Alfred Hart's vocabulary tests, which those who deny Shakespeare's hand in the play have ignored, provide some additional evidence for Shakespeare's part-authorship.[2] He divided the play into two parts – Act I; Act III, Scene I; Act V, Scenes I, III, IV constituting the Shakespearian part – and he demonstrated not merely that the two sections of the play differed from each other, but that the Shakespearian section displayed the same characteristics as those of Shakespeare's last period. The following table, based on two of Hart's, shows the frequency of words not previously used by Shakespeare:

| Play | Previously unused words: 1 word per $x$ lines, where $x =$ | Words new to our Literature, where $x =$ |
|---|---|---|
| *Cymbeline* | 14 | 25 |
| *Winter's Tale* | 13 | 28 |
| *Tempest* | 10 | 18 |
| *Two Noble Kinsmen* (S) | 15 | 16 |
| *Two Noble Kinsmen* (F) | 22 | 42 |

[1] A. C. Bradley, *A Miscellany* (1929), pp. 218–22.
[2] *Shakespeare and the Homilies* (1934), pp. 242 ff.

Hart goes on to show that the coinages by the part-author of *The Two Noble Kinsmen* were the sort of which Shakespeare was fond. More detailed analysis of the vocabulary of Shakespeare's plays needs to be carried out. There is some evidence that the vocabulary of some plays was enlarged by the books Shakespeare happened to be reading at the time. Florio's translation of Montaigne, for example, contributed many words, not before used by Shakespeare, to *King Lear*. In *Troilus and Cressida* Shakespeare not only picked up a number of words from Chapman's Homer (e.g., *emulous, depravation, imbecility, transportance*) but he also introduced into other plays of the period words used by Chapman, and he coined many other words of a similar kind. It is necessary, therefore, to be cautious in applying vocabulary tests to doubtful plays, both because Shakespeare's practice was apt to vary and because we have too little knowledge of the habits of Shakespeare's contemporaries. Nevertheless, Hart's article strengthens the case for Shakespeare's part-authorship of *The Two Noble Kinsmen*.

But it might be argued that there was some other dramatist, known or unknown, who was capable of writing these scenes and able to display by accident or design the same metrical characteristics as Shakespeare. H. D. Sykes claimed [1] that Massinger was the author of the scenes not by Fletcher; but as he also ascribed to Massinger the Shakespearian scenes of *Henry VIII*, his methods would seem to be unreliable. He certainly offers a number of plausible parallels with Massinger's acknowledged work. He compares, for example, 'widdoes to our

[1] *Studies in Shakespeare* (1919), pp. 1–17.

woes' (I. i. 167) with 'marriage of my sorrows' (*Thierry and Theodoret*, IV. ii.); and, more strikingly, Emilia's line (V. i. 141) –

Allow'st no more blood than will make a blush –

with several lines by Massinger:

> if impious acts
> Have left thee blood enough to make a blush.
> (*The Spanish Curate*, III. iii.)

> Thy intent
> To be a whore, leave thee not blood enough
> To make an honest blush.
> (*The Duke of Milan*, IV. iii.)

> the too much praise . . .
> Could not but spring up blushes in my cheeks,
> If grief had left me blood enough to speak
> My humble modesty.
> (*The Parliament of Love*, V. i.)

Quite clearly these quotations are related to each other; yet Massinger was notoriously prone not merely to repeat himself, but also to echo other poets. It is significant that the two leading authorities on Massinger's work, A. K. McIlwraith and A. H. Cruickshank, did not believe that he had a hand in *The Two Noble Kinsmen*.

It is impossible to prove authorship by means of parallels. Many dramatists, including Fletcher and Massinger, are imitative; and they tend to echo their own previous work as well as that of other dramatists. A few

Shakespeare's Hand in

parallels, pointed out in Littledale's edition, will illustrate the difficulties.

A line in the opening song –

> Mary-golds, on death-beds blowing –

may be compared with some lines in *Pericles* (IV. i. 16):

> marigolds
> Shall as a carpet hang upon thy grave
> While summer-days do last.

Shakespeare may be echoing himself; Fletcher may be echoing Shakespeare; or, if there was a custom of planting marigolds on graves, Fletcher or some other dramatist may have hit on the line without knowledge of *Pericles*. In the same song the primrose is described as

> first-borne child of Ver,
> Merry spring-time's herbinger
> With her bels dimme.

Littledale compares the 'faint primrose' in *A Midsummer-Night's Dream* (I. i. 215). Two poets, however, might have arrived at their epithets independently. In the same scene the lines –

> Extremity, that sharpens sundry wits,
> Makes me a foole –

are clearly connected with the lines in *The Honest Man's Fortune* (III. i.):

> Cunning Calamity,
> That others' gross wits uses to refine,
> When I most need it, dulls the edge of mine.

Fletcher (or Massinger) may have been echoing the passage in *The Two Noble Kinsmen*; or the passage in *The Two Noble Kinsmen*, by Fletcher or another, may be echoed from *The Honest Man's Fortune*.

Where there appear to be several echoes from Shakespeare's plays in a short passage, it seems more probable that Shakespeare was the author than that another poet combined echoes from a number of unpublished plays. Arcite's prayer is a case in point:

> Thou mighty one, that with thy power hast turnd
> Greene Neptune into purple; whose approach
> Comets prewarne; whose havocke in vaste feild
> Unearthed skulls proclaims; whose breath blowes downe
> The teeming Ceres' foyzon . . .

The phrase 'Greene Neptune' occurs in *The Winter's Tale* (IV. iv. 28) and the idea of its changing to purple – Senecan in origin – in Macbeth's 'Making the green one red'. The 'vaste feild' recalls the 'vasty fields' in *Henry V* (Prologue); 'unearthed' recalls the use of 'earth'd' in *The Tempest* to mean 'buried'; Ceres in the same play uses the word 'foison', and Lucio in *Measure for Measure* (I. iv. 43) uses the phrase 'teeming foison'.

Another group of multiple echoes is to be found in III. i.

> This is a solemne rite
> They owe bloomd May, and the Athenians pay it
> To th'heart of ceremony. O queene Emilia,
> Fresher then May, sweeter
> Then hir gold buttons on the bowes, or all
> Th'enamelld knackes o'th'mead or garden: yea!

We challenge too the bancke of any nymph,
That makes the streame seeme flowers; thou, O jewell
O'th'wood, o'th'world, hast likewise blest a place
With thy sole presence! In thy rumination
That I, poore man, might eftsoones come betweene,
And chop on some cold thought!

The masque in *The Tempest* affords a number of parallels:[1]

> . . . And flat *meads* thatch'd with stover, them to keep
> Thy *banks* with pioned and twilled brims,
> Which spongy April at thy hest betrims,
> To make *cold nymphs* chaste crowns;

There is a reference to *flowers* and bed-*rite* later in the masque. In *A Midsummer-Night's Dream* (IV. i. 130–40) the month of May is linked, not unnaturally, with *rite*, *solemnity*, wood-*birds*, and *world*; and in *The Merry Wives of Windsor* May is linked with *buttons* (III. ii. 58–9). Arcite's reference to Emilia as

> jewell
> O'th'wood, o'th'world

recalls Imogen's description of her husband as 'jewell in the world', Cerimon's comparison of Thaisa's eyes to 'heavenly jewels' which 'make the world twice rich', and the widespread jewel imagery in the plays of the last period.

[1] The presence of internal rhyme in the *Two Noble Kinsmen* passage (*stream/seem*; *chop/drop*) suggests that it may originally have been, like *The Tempest* masque, in rhymed couplets:

> That I
> Poor man, might eftsoons come between and chop
> On some cold thought! thrice-blessed chance, to drop
> On such a mistress. . . .

But such echoes are not in themselves proof of Shakespeare's authorship. They might conceivably be by a clever anonymous imitator; or, since there is nothing surprising in the associations, the resemblances may be fortuitous. It is only when the associations are strange and unusual that they may be said to throw a convincing light on authorship.

Caroline Spurgeon discussed the possibility of determining authorship by a study of imagery; and the most enlightening study [1] of *The Two Noble Kinsmen* from this point of view is that by M. Mincoff. He points out, for example, that the author of the 'Shakespearian' scenes of the play exhibits the poet's characteristic love of nature. Although, as he says, 'the richness depends as much on force, complexity, depth of development, as on actual frequency', it may be worth mentioning that a high proportion of the imagery is drawn from nature, nearly a quarter. Mincoff gives examples of images of growth and ripening, river images, and images of swimming, of images relating to the feel of substances, of sensitiveness to decaying corpses, or concrete vividness of personifications – all characteristic of Shakespeare – and even of a running image (I. i. 75, 116, 167, 240). The author of these scenes shows another characteristic mark of Shakespeare's style, a rapid dissolving of one image into the next, as in the lines –

> O my petition was
> Set downe in yce, which by hot greefe uncandied
> Melts into drops, so sorrow, wanting forme,
> Is prest with deeper matter.

[1] *English Studies* (1952), pp. 97 ff.

Here 'the idea of melting drops of ice turns to drops of wax and the impression of a seal'.

To these points may be added two others. Like Shakespeare, the author of these scenes sometimes links his images together by puns, as in the description of Palamon (V. iii. 46):

> Palamon
> Has a most menacing aspect; his brow
> Is *grav'd*, and seemes to *bury* what it frownes on.

The other point reinforces the fact that the play was written by two dramatists, and fits in with the assumption that one of the authors was Shakespeare: the fields from which the imagery is drawn in the two parts of the play show some striking differences. There is less imagery drawn from nature in the Fletcher scenes, much less from business and wealth, and none at all from sickness and medicine. The other poet has no fewer than seventeen images derived from sickness and medicine: e.g.,

> cure their surfeit
> That craves a present medcine ... (I. i. 191)

> Thou purger of the earth ... (I. i. 48)

> that peace might purge
> For her repletion ... (I. ii. 23)

> almost puts
> Faith in a feavour ... (I. ii. 66)

> that heal'st with blood
> The earth when it is sicke, and cur'st the world
> O' the pluresie of people ... (V. i. 64)

In spite, however, of the number of disease images, they are not easy to interpret. They help to create the atmosphere of a diseased society which can be cured only by war; and they contrast with the nature images centred on Emilia. In Palamon's address to Venus love and disease are juxtaposed (see below p. 142). But perhaps the iteration of Fortune – nine times in the non-Fletcherian scenes – and the thirty-six references to the Gods have more significance. The sudden changes of fortune and the apparently incomprehensible behaviour of the gods form the main theme of the play. Theseus enunciates the moral:

> O you heavenly charmers,
> What things you make of us! For what we lacke
> We laugh, for what we have, are sorry; still
> Are children in some kind. Let us be thankfull
> For that which is, and with you leave dispute
> That are above our question.

Mincoff is right to maintain that

> No author has been, or can be suggested whose style approaches that of the doubtful parts of *The Two Noble Kinsmen* even approximately as closely as Shakespeare's does. On the internal evidence alone Shakespeare remains the only possible candidate. The idea of an epigone, unschooled in philological analysis, imitating the minutiae of Shakespeare's style at a definite period down to the very metrical percentages, capable too of such splendid poetry, yet never, apparently, repeating the attempt, is too fanciful to need refutation.

Whether the evidence so far offered for the Shakespearian authorship of parts of *The Two Noble Kinsmen* amounts to positive proof is a matter of opinion. The case seems to me to be so strong that the onus of proof really rests on the sceptics; but some good critics still cling to the idea of this anonymous imitator. One of these was Professor Una Ellis-Fermor. She delivered a paper on the subject at the Shakespeare Survey Conference in 1949, and in her copy of *The Shakespeare Apocrypha*, now in the Shakespeare Institute Library, there are a number of interesting notes in her handwriting. She admits that the opening scene of the play is great poetry, 'as far as style can make it', that the author has caught Shakespeare's music to a miracle, that his imagery is brilliant, that he writes in a masterful and mature style, like Shakespeare's latest, that he is not a mere imitator, the Shakespearian echoes being imaginatively reproduced; but, she argues, the imagery is too consistently brilliant, the style is not subordinated to the needs of the play, and the brilliance is 'like underpainting with white. Shakespeare does not do this continuously – only when dramatically relevant'. She notes that one scene contains 'speech after speech of matchless poetry – or rather rhetoric'.

Professor Ellis-Fermor wrote these comments before the publication of recent studies of the imagery of the play, and she did, indeed, mention the need of such studies. But I find it impossible to believe in an unknown poet who wrote great poetry, only distinguishable from Shakespeare's by its excess and continuity of brilliance. Such masterly ease and assurance could be achieved only at the end of a career, not at the beginning of an abortive one; and the author of these scenes, if not Shakespeare, has left no mark on the drama of his time. Nor, I think, should we accept too easy a distinction between poetry and rhetoric. If by rhetoric Professor Ellis-Fermor meant to imply a lack of sincerity or of genuine feeling, it may be mentioned that De Quincey, who likewise distinguished between poetry and rhetoric, came to a very different conclusion about the play. He declared that in the first and last acts,

> which, in point of composition, is perhaps the most superb work in the language . . . would have been the most gorgeous rhetoric, had they not happened to be something far better.

The best episodes

> are finished in a more elaborate style of excellence than any other almost of Shakespeare's most felicitous scenes. In their first intention they were perhaps merely rhetorical; but the furnace of composition has transmuted their substance.

Let us assume, however, that this anonymous imitator of Shakespeare did exist. He was (let us say) a young poet of the name of Henry Tomkins who came up to London to study at one of the Inns of Court, and spent all his time in the playhouse, watching Shakespeare's plays. He bribed the prompter to lend him copies of *The Tempest* and *The Winter's Tale*, and began to write *The Two Noble Kinsmen*. He took a few scenes to Burbage, who thought they were promising enough to get Fletcher to collaborate. When Burbage, noticing the Shakespearian flavour of Tomkins's style, asked him how he managed it, the young man explained modestly his methods of composition. He had always admired Shakespeare's work and he had tried to imitate it as closely as possible. He had counted up the percentage of weak-endings and light-endings in his last few plays and had kept to this percentage in his own verse – or rather he had increased the percentage to tally with what Shakespeare might have written in 1613. He had noticed that Shakespeare introduced a word he had not used before every twelve lines and a new coinage every twenty lines; but he decided to coin a new word rather more frequently, since the percentage tended to increase. He had been careful, of course, to draw his images from the same fields as Shakespeare, and in roughly the same proportion. The reason why we hear nothing of Tomkins is that he died of the plague a few months later.

I find it very hard to believe in Tomkins; and even if it were possible to swallow all the above improbabilities, there remains a still more difficult obstacle for believers, a yet smaller needle's eye for the camel to get through. How did Tomkins manage, three hundred years in advance of his age, to penetrate the mysteries of Shakespeare's unconscious mind and to unravel its unconscious associations without the benefit of a concordance? How did he come to use the same image-clusters as Shakespeare?

Edward A. Armstrong, as we have seen, suggested in *Shakespeare's Imagination* that image-clusters might be used as an aid to the authentication of Shakespeare's work:

> Cluster criticism provides a powerful auxiliary weapon for the critic's armoury, but like every weapon it has to be used with discretion. ... It would be deplorable if cluster criticism were to be regarded as in any way superseding other techniques or if its possibilities were to be so exaggerated as to bring its legitimate applications into discredit.

Armstrong then refers to *The Two Noble Kinsmen*, and he says that examination of a few clusters in that play gives 'no conclusive support' to the claim that Shakespeare was responsible for parts of it; on the contrary, 'it seems more probable that Shakespeare's influence rather than his handiwork is perceptible in it'.[1] It is, I believe, possible to question the validity of this conclusion, and to show that Shakespeare's hand is indeed perceptible in some scenes of the play.

Some clusters, of course, are not peculiar to Shakespeare. Poets with approximately the same environment may be expected to have the same associations for particular words. It is not surprising even that the graduate Marlowe and the grammar-school product, Shakespeare, should have at least one cluster in common. The most convincing proof would be offered by the presence of clusters the parts of which are not logically associated and which have not been found in the work of other poets, as with the Hum cluster discussed below (p. 118).

Mr Armstrong does not mention which clusters in *The Two Noble Kinsmen* he has examined; but we may readily admit that there are some which can throw no light on authorship. Shakespeare, for example, associates *snow* with *chastity* and *Diana*, and indirectly with *heat*, *blood*, and *blush*.[2] But these associations are too obvious to have any significance by themselves.

> Look thou be true; do not give dalliance
> Too much the rein; the strongest oaths are straw

[1] *Op. cit.*, p. 188.
[2] Cf. *Tempest*, IV. i. 55; *Coriolanus*, V. iii. 66; *Timon*, IV. iii. 386; *Cymbeline*, II. v. 13.

To th'fire i'th'blood. Be more abstemious,
Or else good night your vow!
    I warrant you, sir,
The white cold virgin snow upon my heart
Abates the ardour of my liver.

The moon of Rome, chaste as the icicle
That's curdied by the frost from purest snow,
And hangs on Dian's temple – dear Valeria!

Thou ever young, fresh, lov'd, and delicate wooer,
Whose blush doth thaw the consecrated snow
That lies on Dian's lap!

    my mother seem'd
The Dian of that time. So doth my wife
The nonpareil of this . . .
Me of my lawful pleasure she restrain'd,
And pray'd me oft forbearance; did it with
A pudency so rosy, the sweet view on't
Might well have warm'd old Saturn; that I thought her
As chaste as unsunn'd snow.

The presence of the same associations in *The Two Noble Kinsmen* (V. i.) cannot in itself be taken to prove that Shakespeare wrote this scene. Emilia prays to *Diana*:

O sacred, shadowie, cold and constant queene,
Abandoner of revells, mute, contemplative,
Sweet, solitary, white as chaste, and pure
As winde-fand snow, who to thy female knights
Allow'st no more blood than will make a blush,
Which is their order's robe.

There is, however, a closer parallel to this passage in *The Winter's Tale* (IV. iv. 373–6), as Littledale pointed out:

> I take thy hand, this hand,
> As soft as dove's down and as *pure* as it,
> Or Ethiopian's tooth, or the *fann'd snow* that's bolted
> By the northern *blasts* twice o'er.

It seems fairly certain that the lines in *The Two Noble Kinsmen* were written either by a conscious imitator of Shakespeare or by Shakespeare himself. None of the plays quoted above had appeared in print by the time *The Two Noble Kinsmen* was written, though a playgoer could have remembered and imitated the passages concerned.

Another cluster, for the discovery of which I am indebted to a former pupil, links the Hind with dirt, smell, lust, disease, crime, and death.[1] In the same scene of *The Two Noble Kinsmen* a silver hind is carried before Emilia, 'in which is conveyed incense and sweet *odours*'; and in the speech from which lines have been quoted above there are references to dirt (145 *maculate*), lust (147 *scurrill, wanton*), crime (154 *guiltlesse*), and death (156 *doombe*). For the remaining link in the chain, disease, we have to go back to Palamon's speech, which has a nice selection of diseases (110 *crampe*, 112 *gout*, 113 *convulsions*). Unless it could be shown that some other dramatist shares these associations, there is strong reason to believe

[1] Cf. F. D. Gibson, *Sport in Shakespeare* (Thesis in Library of University of Leeds). Cf., e.g., *Richard III*, II. iv. 50–3; *Comedy of Errors*, III. i. 74–88; *Midsummer-Night's Dream*, II. i. 232–7; *As You Like It*, III. ii. 102–14; *Troilus and Cressida*, III. ii. 185–93; *Merry Wives*, III. v. 87–93; *All's Well*, I. i. 90–2; *Julius Caesar*, I. iii. 106–11.

that Shakespeare wrote this scene, and, of course, it is a scene which has been ascribed to Shakespeare on quite other grounds.

Another scene which is thought by many critics to be Shakespearian is the first in the play. Here is to be found (108) the unusual word 'uncandied' – a word which inevitably recalls 'Discandying' and 'discandy', both used by Shakespeare in *Antony and Cleopatra*. In one case (III. xiii.) the word is associated with *cold, hail, dissolve,*[1] *drop, heart, moon, graveless,* and *Nile* (153–66); and in the other case (IV. xii.) with *melt, heart,* and *sun* (18–28). In *The Two Noble Kinsmen* the Second Queen complains that her lord is unburied (cf. *graveless*) –

> Showing the *sun* his teeth, grinning at the *moone*.

Hippolyta uses the word '*heart*-deepe'; and the Third Queen says (106–12):

> O, my petition was
> Set downe in *yce*, which, by hot greefe *uncandied*,
> *Melts* into *drops* . . .
> You cannot reade it there; there through my teares,
> Like wrinckled pebbles in a glassie streame
> You may behold 'em!

The second of the passages from *Antony and Cleopatra* contains that most famous of image-clusters, flatterers–dogs–sweets; and it might perhaps be regarded as an argument against the authenticity of *The Two Noble Kinsmen* passage that there is no mention of either

[1] Littledale points out that the phrase 'dissolve my life' appears both in this passage and in *The Two Noble Kinsmen*, III. ii. 20 (apparently by Fletcher).

flatterers or sweets. But although other uses of *candied* (e.g., *Timon*, IV. iii. 226 and *Hamlet*, III. ii. 65) are linked with that cluster, there are no dogs – though there are flatterers – in the other *Antony and Cleopatra* passage, and neither dog nor flatterer in *The Tempest* context (II. i. 279). It is as though Shakespeare had worked the dogs and the flatterers out of his system in the great purge of *Timon of Athens*, the play in which this particular cluster is the iterative image.

The case of the Osprey is also significant. In *Coriolanus* (IV. vii.) Aufidius describes the hero's march on Rome:

> I think he'll be to Rome
> As is the osprey to the fish, who take it
> By sovereignty of nature.

So in *The Two Noble Kinsmen* (I. i. again) the First Queen tells Theseus:

> your actions,
> Soone as they moove, as asprayes doe the fish,
> Subdue before they touch.

It might be said that two authors derived their knowledge of the osprey from a common source were it not for the contexts of the two passages. In *Coriolanus* there are references to *war* (45), *breaking the neck* (25), *sword* (24), *lord* (41), and *sovereignty* (35); and more remotely to *tomb* (52), *darkened* (5), and *action* (5). In *The Two Noble Kinsmen* context there are references to *war* (133), *cords* (142), *knives* [1]

---

[1] Littledale compares 'cords, knives, drams, precipitance' with *Othello*, III. iii. 386:

> If there be cords or knives
> Poison or fire, or suffocating streams.

(142), *lords* (141), *Kings* (139), *beds*=graves (140), *graves* (150), *shadows* (145), and *actions* (135). It might be argued that the author of the latter passage had consciously echoed the lines about the osprey from an unpublished play, and that he had unconsciously echoed some of the key words in the same context. But such an argument strains our credulity, and it is much more likely that the same poet wrote both passages.

This probability is raised to a certainty when we turn to yet another cluster in the same scene [1] – perhaps Armstrong's most impressive cluster. He detailed all the fourteen references to Kites by Shakespeare and showed that in nearly every context there are references to death, food, spirits, bed and other birds, and that in every context there are references to three or more of these associations. There are the same associations with *hell-kite* in *Macbeth* IV. iii., a passage to which Armstrong does not refer. As these associations are invariable with Shakespeare, their absence in a doubtful scene would almost be sufficient to prove that Shakespeare did not write it. But the mention of kites (41) in the first scene of *The Two Noble Kinsmen* is at the centre of the same cluster in its entirety – *ravens* (41), *crows* (42), *dead* (50), *slain* (47), *bed* (30), *angel* (16), *pie* (21), and *devour* (70).

Another image-cluster analysed by Armstrong is that associated with the word 'hum'. When the word was first used by Shakespeare in *1 Henry IV* (III. i. 158) it was linked with food (*cates*), music (*ballad-monger*), wealth (*mines of India*), and spirit (*devil*), but not with sleep or death. A year or two later, in *The Merry Wives of Windsor*

[1] Cf. K. Muir, *N.Q.* (1954), pp. 52–3.

(III. v. 141), Shakespeare used the word again, this time linked with *sleep*, *devil*, and *cuckold*. He used it twice in *Henry V*: in one context linked with *drowsy* and *ghost* (IV. Prol.), in the other with *executors*, *honey*, *yawning*, *singing*, *flower-buds*, and *gold* (I. ii. 202). In *Hamlet* (V. i.) the word is linked with *skull*, *tricks*, and *inheritance*; and there is an earlier example in *Hamlet* (II. ii. 584) – overlooked by Armstrong because it is a Second Quarto reading omitted from the Globe text and the Bartlett *Concordance* – where the word is accompanied by most of the usual associations, *offal* (food), *spirit*, *murder* (death), *John a Dreams* (sleep), *ears*, *bawdy*, and *lecherous* (adultery), and the plot to catch the conscience of the King. In *Othello* (V. ii. 39) the word is associated with *kill*, *gnaw*, *bed*, *rose*, *spirit*, and *adultery* – harking back to the *cuckold* of *The Merry Wives* and *lecherous* in *Hamlet*. (The murder of Desdemona is, of course, the culmination of Iago's *plot*.) In *King Lear* the word is linked with Edgar's supposed plot to kill Gloucester, with *conspiracy*, *taste*, *relish*, *sleep*, *note*, *sounded*, and *revenue*. Edmund, moreover, is the fruit of adultery. The word is used three times in *Macbeth*: in Act III, Scene II it is linked with *treason*, *meal*, *drowse*, *yawning*, *peal*, *note*, *Hecate* (for *spirit*) and *copy* (possibly standing for *wealth*). The killing of Banquo is being discussed in the context. In Act III, Scene VI the word is linked with *kill*, *feasts*, *meat*, *sleep*, and *angel*, and the characters are virtually plotting against Macbeth. In Act IV, Scene III the word is linked with *slaughter*, *deer*, *sound*, *tune*, *precious*, *ears* and *fiend*. In *Cymbeline* (III. v. 104) the word is linked only with *dead*, though Cloten hatches his plot soon afterwards, and he uses the words *fiends* and *dined*. In *The*

*Winter's Tale* (II. i. 71) it is linked with *bed*, with Hermione's supposed adultery, and with the plot to kill
Polixenes. In *The Tempest* (III. ii. 132) the word is linked
with *kill*, *plot*, *sleep*, *sounds*, *airs*, *music*, *song*, *riches*, *ears*, *Ariel*
(a spirit), and with the product of miscegenation, Caliban.
By the end of Shakespeare's career, therefore, *hum* had
picked up a whole cluster of associations – some of
which are not mentioned by Armstrong and most of
which are unexpected – and any use of the word after 1610
would be likely to evoke some of the following associations: death, plot, food, sleep, music, song, flowers,
wealth or value, ears, spirit, adultery or bastardy. Of these
eleven associations all but one – plot – duly make their
appearance in the context of the sole use of the word in
*The Two Noble Kinsmen* (I. iii. 75):

> the *flowre* that I would plucke
> And put betweene my breasts, O – then but beginning
> To swell about the *blossome* – she would long
> Till she had such another: and commit it
> To the like innocent cradle, where Phoenix-like,
> They *dide* in perfume; on my head no toy
> But was her patterne; her affections – pretty,
> Though happely her careless wear – I followed
> For my most serious decking; had mine *eare*
> Stolne some new *aire*, or at adventure *humd* one
> From *musicall coynadge*, why, it was a *note*
> Whereon her *spirits* would sojourne, – rather dwell on, –
> And *sing* it in her *slumbers*: this rehearsall –
> Which, ev'ry innocent wots well, comes in
> Like old importments *bastard* – has this end,
> That the true love tweene mayde and mayde may be
> More then in sex dividuall.

## The Two Noble Kinsmen

A few lines later Hippolyta speaks of 'a sickely appetite'. (Perhaps the word immediately before this quotation, 'arraignement', may serve as a substitute for *plot*: Shakespeare uses *arraign* on eight occasions, and on six of these in connexion with treason.[1]) Ten of these associations occur within fifteen lines, and the remaining one is only eight lines later. It is difficult to believe that Shakespeare was conscious of these associations, or that one of his imitators would have stumbled on so many of them. It can hardly be denied that Shakespeare wrote this scene too. It so happens that the word *hum* is used also in one of the Fletcher scenes (III. v.), but here it is accompanied by none of the Shakespearian associations. Three other words which are the nodal points of Shakespearian clusters are to be found in Fletcher scenes – *Venison* [2] (III. iii.), *Hawk* (II. v., III. v.), *Bark* (III. v.) – but in none of these cases is there any sign of the accompanying clusters.

There appear to be no Shakespearian image-clusters in the remaining scenes of the play, but this does not necessarily mean that he had no hand in them. Only a few clusters have so far been isolated; and most of these, owing to the fact that Armstrong is an ornithologist, are connected with birds. In the plays of the last period – excluding *Pericles* and *Henry VIII* – only twelve clusters have been discovered. As no one pretends that Shakespeare wrote more than half of *The Two Noble Kinsmen*, it

[1] Laertes's rebellion (*Hamlet*, IV. v. 90), Lear's arraignment of Goneril (*King Lear*, III. vi. 46), Goneril's claim that the laws are hers (*King Lear*, V. iii. 159), and the trial of Hermione for high treason (*Winter's Tale*, II. iii. 201).

[2] *Venison* and *Hawk* clusters have been analysed by Gibson, *op. cit.* I have searched in vain for image-clusters in Massinger's plays.

would be sanguine to expect more than one or two clusters in the authentic scenes. Yet, as we have seen, in addition to two of the Armstrong clusters (*kite* and *hum*) there are two or three others present in the first and third scenes of the first act and the first scene of the fifth. If the reader admits Shakespeare's hand in these scenes he is not likely to doubt that Shakespeare was responsible for other scenes as well. The various tests which have been applied (weak endings, light endings, scene endings, coinages) all receive reinforcement from a proof on imagistic grounds that Shakespeare wrote even part of a single scene. Since we have seen that Shakespeare wrote parts of three separate scenes, the evidence of other tests, together with the convictions of Coleridge, Bradley, Theodore Spencer, and Middleton Murry, make it reasonably certain that Shakespeare wrote also the following scenes: I. ii., I. iv., III. i., V. iv. The play has as much right to be included in editions of Shakespeare as *Sir Thomas More* or *The Passionate Pilgrim*, and perhaps as much as *Titus Andronicus*, *1 Henry VI*, and *Pericles*.[1]

[1] Frederick O. Waller, *Studies in Bibliography*, XI (1958), pp. 61–84, has examined the 1634 quarto for bibliographical evidences of authorship. The occurrence of '*em* and *ye* (with other words and spellings characteristic of Fletcher) makes him divide the play between Fletcher and his collaborator in much the same proportions as previous critics have done; but he ascribes some scenes, of which on other grounds the authorship is doubtful, to Shakespeare (II. i., III. ii.) and he gives to Fletcher a few lines in Shakespearian scenes (i.e., I. i. 25–8, I. iv. 22–38, V. i. 1–17, V. iv. 22–38). These insertions, he thinks, were made by Fletcher when he was preparing the play for the stage. He argues that the rate of occurrence of various contractions 'in the non-Fletcherian scenes . . . identifies these scenes as Shakespeare's'. He finds evidence of more archaic spellings

in the Shakespearian scenes, and this would at least support the view that Fletcher's collaborator was an older man. He also argues from the textual tangles and general carelessness in the Shakespearian scenes that they were less finished than Fletcher's.

It is useful to have yet another confirmation of the dual authorship of the play and of Shakespeare's probable authorship of certain scenes. Mr Waller, perhaps, goes further than the bibliographical evidence will warrant in his positive statements of Shakespeare's authorship, and it is difficult to be sure of the authorship of the two short scenes he wishes to add to the canon.

# VII

# *The Two Noble Kinsmen*

*The Two Noble Kinsmen* begins where *A Midsummer-Night's Dream* ends – with the marriage of Theseus and Hippolyta. Eighteen years or more separate the two plays, and the stage had changed a good deal in the interval. The influence of the private theatres and the splendour of Court masques is apparent in some of Shakespeare's last plays. The only entertainment provided for Duke Theseus on his wedding day is a performance by some not very talented actors of the tragedy of Pyramus and Thisbe. The opening stage-direction in *The Two Noble Kinsmen* illustrates the difference:

> Enter Hymen with a Torch burning; a Boy in a white Robe, singing and strewing Flowres; after Hymen, a Nimph, encompast in her Tresses, bearing a wheaten Garland; then Theseus, between two other Nimphs with wheaten Chaplets on their heades; then Hipolita, the Bride, led by Pirithous, and another holding a Garland over her head (*her Tresses likewise hanging*). After her, Emilia, holding up her Train. (*Artesius and Attendants.*)

Immediately after the singing of the very beautiful bridal song – 'Roses their sharp spines being gone' – which Dowden and others ascribe to Fletcher, the ceremonies are interrupted by the appearance of three Queenes, in Blacke, with vailes staind, with imperiall Crownes. The first Queene fals downe at the foote of Theseus; The second fals downe at the foote of Hypolita; The third before Emilia.

The pleading of the three queens whose husbands lie unburied at the order of Creon is much more effective than it is in the source, *The Knight's Tale* of Chaucer, where instead of three queens speaking antiphonally we have a whole procession of women with a single spokeswoman. Chaucer's Theseus, moreover, is already married to Hippolyta, and he needs no persuading to make war on Creon. In the play the ceremony is not yet over, and Theseus, though ready to set out on a campaign, wants at first to finish his wedding. He is persuaded by his bride and Emilia to postpone the ceremony until after his campaign. The only characteristic which distinguishes Theseus from any heroic figure is that he is continually revoking his firm decisions at the wish of his women-folk. He carries a stage further what has often been observed in the characters of Shakespeare's final period – a tendency to flattening and conventionality which we do not get in the comedies and tragedies written between 1597 and 1607.

But, in fact, this first scene does not require profound or subtle characterization. It requires only an eloquent treatment of the initial situation – the mourning queens interrupting the wedding – and it would be inappropriate for the characters to be individualized. Within this convention the whole scene is written with masterly ease and assurance. Shakespeare has developed one stage further the elaborate syntax and subtle rhythms to be found in

*The Winter's Tale* and *Cymbeline*, so that we almost forget that we are listening to verse. Take, for example, the Second Queen's appeal to Hippolyta. The speech is twenty-four lines long, and it consists of a single periodic sentence. It never gives the impression, as some of the speeches in *Troilus and Cressida* do, of a set oration; but each clause follows naturally, and without premeditation, from the one before:

> Honoured Hypolita,
> Most dreaded *Amazonian*, that hast slaine
> The Sith-tuskd Bore; that, with thy Arme as strong
> As it is white, wast neere to make the male
> To thy Sex captive, but that this thy Lord,
> Borne to uphold Creation in that honour
> First Nature stilde it in, shrunke thee into
> The bownd thou wast ore-flowing, at once subduing
> Thy force, and thy affection; Soldiresse,
> That equally canst poize sternnes with pitty;
> Who now I know hast much more power on him
> Than ever he had on thee; who ow'st his strength
> And his Love too, who is a Servant for
> The Tenour of thy Speech; Deere Glasse of Ladies,
> Bid him that we, whom flaming war doth scortch,
> Vnder the shaddow of his Sword may coole us:
> Require him he advance it ore our heades;
> Speak't in a womans key: like such a woman
> As any of us three; weepe ere you faile;
> Lend us a knee;
> But touch the ground for us no longer time
> Than a Doves motion, when the head's pluckt off:
> Tell him, if he i' the blood cizd field lay swolne,
> Showing the sun his Teeth, grinning at the Moone.
> What you would doe.

Emilia is one of the most prominent characters in the first scene. In the second we are introduced to the prospective rivals for her love, the two noble kinsmen. Here Shakespeare is less successful than he had been in the first scene, where characterization is of secondary importance, for the twin heroes are as indistinguishable as Tweedledum and Tweedledee. They both complain of the morals and manners of Thebes, of the treatment of veterans, of the low wages given for honourable toil, of fashions in dress, and of the evil tyranny of their uncle, Creon; and they both agree that notwithstanding their realization of the justice of Theseus's attack on Thebes, they must fight for their native city. The function of the scene is presumably to show that Palamon and Arcite, although Thebans, are honourable, and worthy of Emilia's love; but although Shakespeare's verse remains skilful, the general impression of the scene is one of perfunctoriness.

The third scene is designed to amplify the character of Emilia by a conversation with Hippolyta in which the masculine friendship of Theseus and Pirithous is compared with the childish love of Emilia for the dead Flavina. Emilia's long speech about Flavina – consisting of a remarkable complex sentence of twenty-eight lines – is a beautiful piece of self-characterization; and her conviction that she will never love a man as much as she loved the dead child is an excellent preparation for the chief difficulty of the story – the fact that Emilia seems unable to choose between Palamon and Arcite. The speech is also important because friendship and loyalty constitute one of the main themes of the play. In addition to the two friendships just mentioned, there is the central friendship, threatened by love, of the two noble kinsmen; their loyalty to Thebes; and the loyalty of their followers, who willingly consent to die with them, in the last act.

The fourth scene is concerned with Theseus's victory and the taking prisoner of the desperately wounded friends. The fifth scene, dealing with the funeral of the three kings, provides another opportunity for music and pageantry, appreciated by the patrons of the Blackfriars Theatre. It is not certain, however, whether these two short scenes are Shakespeare or Fletcher's – one line of the song 'And clamours through the wild air flying' was the inspiration of one of the songs in Tennyson's *Princess* – but they round off the theme of the unburied kings, and they are in keeping with the rest of the act.

The play, up to this point, has obviously been well planned and well written. Theodore Spencer, in his valuable article on the play, while admitting the superb rhetoric of parts of the first and third scenes, complained that the writing was tired, the muscles behind it slack and old. It seems to me, on the contrary, that there is no sign of tiredness or flabbiness in the actual writing. One does not feel, as one often does in comparing Mr Eliot's later plays, *The Confidential Clerk* or *The Elder Statesman* with *Murder in the Cathedral* or *The Family Reunion*, that his imagination has become blunted and that he is relying on ever feebler echoes of his former triumphs. Only in the characterization does there seem to be a definite falling off – a process that had begun with *Pericles* – though we may say with Mr Eliot that Shakespeare in his final plays was seeing through the actions of men into a spiritual action which transcended them.

In addition to the friendship theme which I have mentioned, Shakespeare states two other themes in the first act of the play – the power of fortune and the inscrutable workings of the Gods. Fortune is referred to many times. When Theseus first beheld the young bride of King Capaneus, Fortune, at her 'Dimpled her cheek with smiles'; and looking on her in her widowed state he observes:

> O greife and time
> Fearefull consumers, you will all devoure.

In the second scene we are told that the villainy of Creon

> almost puts
> Faith in a feavour, and deifies alone
> Voluble chance.

Fortune, it appears, becomes a goddess, only through man's frailty. But at the end of the scene Arcite submits all to the event, 'that never-erring Arbitratour'; and he tells Palamon:

> Let us follow
> The becking of our chance.

In the third scene Hippolyta wishes Thesus power 'To dare ill-dealing Fortune'; and at the end of the scene she prays not *to* Fortune, but for his fortunes.

The references to the gods are equally significant, and they are plainly designed to prepare the way for the great invocations of Mars, Venus, and Diana which were the climax of Chaucer's tale. There are several references to Phoebus, Juno, Hercules, Hymen, and Bellona, and a large number to Jupiter, Mars, and the gods in general. Perhaps the most interesting are those which suggest that mercy is infused in man by some god; that Theseus is superior to Mars because, although mortal, he can make his affections bend to godlike honours; that earthly injustice deafens the ears of heavenly justice; and that

> Th'imparciall Gods, who from the mounted heavens
> View us their mortall Heard, behold who erre,
> And in their time chastice.

In Act II, which is almost certainly Fletcher's work, and again in the parts of Acts III and IV, which are not Shakespeare's, there is a sudden cessation of references to fortune and the gods, except for a few conventional ones to the 'red-eyed god of war', 'ever-blinded fortune', and Diana. In the Shakespearian scene at the beginning of Act III Arcite speaks of Lady Fortune as 'next after Emily my sovereign'; and in the last scene of the play the First Knight says that Fortune's title is momentary; the Second Knight declares that 'tottering Fortune . . . at her certain'st, reels'; Theseus, on hearing of Arcite's death, says that 'Never Fortune did play a subtler game'; and there are many references to the gods, apart from the great invocations which I shall discuss later.

It is usually said that the thirteen Fletcher scenes in the middle of the play, though manifestly inferior poetically to Shakespeare's, display his usual sense of the theatre. This is true in the sense that individual scenes are effective, but some of them are much less effective than one might have expected. The underplot of the love of the jailer's daughter for Palamon, which offers plenty of opportunity for the kind of pathos of which Fletcher is a master, seems to me to be bungled. The prose scene in which the daughter's love is revealed by her praise of the prisoners is effective enough, though neither she nor her father is given much depth. Fletcher does not often use prose in his plays, and for that reason the scene is sometimes ascribed to Beaumont or Shakespeare. Perhaps the strongest argument against Fletcher's authorship is that the rather mannered prose seems not to suit the character of the simple girl depicted later in the play:

> I doe thinke they have patience to make any adversity ashamd . . . I mervaile how they would have lookd, had they beene Victors, that with such a constant Nobility enforce a freedome out of Bondage, making misery their mirth, and affliction a toy to jest at . . . Yet sometime a devided sigh, martyrd as 'twere i' the deliverance, will breake from one of them; when the other presently gives it so sweete a rebuke, that I could wish my selfe a Sigh to be so chid, or at least a Sigher to be comforted.

Oddly enough, in view of his fondness for scenes between lords and low-born girls, Fletcher does not write a scene between the girl and Palamon – we only hear of their meeting. Instead we are given four scenes consisting of the girl's soliloquies, all in verse. In the first she decides to set him free, in the hope that he will take her as his mistress; in the second she announces that she has set him free; in the third she fails to find him in the forest, and her wits begin to unsettle; and in the fourth scene she comes on mad. The verse of the four soliloquies does not vary its even flow even when the girl is mad, and the total effect is one of monotony and repetition.

> Good night, good night; y'are gone – I'm very hungry.
> Would I could find a fine Frog! he would tell me
> News from all parts o' the world; then would I make
> A Carecke of a Cockle shell, and sayle
> By east and North East to the King of *Pigmes*,
> For he tels fortunes rarely.

This is not how mad people speak; it is not even a literary correlative of such speech; it is a sentimental and feeble substitute for it.

It is usually said that the jailer's daughter is a crude imitation of Ophelia, but apart from the fact that both girls are crossed in love and sing snatches of song, and both play with flowers by a stream, there is really very little resemblance. Fletcher's fault is not that of plagiarism. Nor, I think, should we complain (as the older critics inevitably did) of the lack of maidenly modesty in a girl so much in love that she wants Palamon without a wedding-ring, or of the alleged indecency when the doctor advises her young man to pretend to be Palamon and to lie with her as a means of curing her madness. What we can reasonably complain of, apart from the monotony I have just mentioned, and Fletcher's avoidance of a scene between Palamon and the girl, are the artificiality and unreality of the mad speeches, the way in which the madness is used to arouse laughter, and the disparity between the speaker of courtly prose in Act II and the girl in Act V who has one 'poor petticoat and two coarse smocks'.

There are other inconsistencies. In Act IV we are told that Palamon has given a sum of money for the girl's dowry; and in Act IV he gives his purse to the jailer for the same purpose. This is usually thought to be an addition by Fletcher to a Shakespearian scene, but it seems more likely to be Shakespeare himself writing in ignorance of Fletcher's previous scene.

Every reader will notice the transformation of Palamon and Arcite in Act II. Instead of being the disillusioned social critics of Act I – haunted, as Theodore Spencer put it, by the ghost of Timon; haunted at least by the ghosts of contemporary commentators and satirists – they appear as elegant, sentimental figures who have obviously never brooded on social questions. Thebes, no longer decadent, is described as noble. It is true that in one of Palamon's speeches he speaks of the court of Creon,

> Where sin is Iustice, lust and ignorance
> The vertues of the great ones;

and declares that

> all those pleasures
> That wooe the wils of men to vanity
> I see through now.

But the implication is that he has been brought to this state of mind since his imprisonment. Another obvious discrepancy is to be found in Act III, Scene III, where Palamon and Arcite rally each other on their previous love-affairs. This conflicts with Palamon's prayer to

Venus, in which, with obvious sincerity, he contrasts his chaste conduct with that of libertines.

There is a sudden drop in poetic quality in the prison scene. The rhythm becomes flabbier, the language and imagery more conventional. In place of vivid metaphors we get rather tired similes. Ladies are like tall ships under sail, horses like proud seas under us, people draw their swords like lightning, children are like young eagles, and angry swine fly like a Parthian quiver. Worse still, the images are sometimes confused, not as Shakespeare's are, because one follows so hard on the heels of another, but because Fletcher has not visualized them clearly. Arcite speaks of the disadvantages of prison:

> The sweet embraces of a loving wife,
> Loden with kisses, armd with thousand Cupids,
> Shall never claspe our neckes.

An embrace can hardly be loaden with kisses, or armed with Cupids, and it is the wife, not the embrace, which clasps their necks. In addition to these faults, there are traces of downright vulgarity, as when Palamon, after the departure of Arcite, remarks:

> Were I at liberty, I would doe things
> Of such a vertuous greatnes, that this Lady,
> This blushing virgine, should take manhood to her,
> And seeke to ravish me.

But, in its way, the scene is theatrically effective, if one is not too particular about the texture of the dialogue. It has movement and development. The friends begin by lamenting the disadvantages of imprisonment; they con-

sole themselves by the thought that at least they can never
be separated, as they might if they were free; and they
vow eternal friendship. Just before the appearance of
Emilia Palamon declares:

> I do not think it possible our friendship
> Should ever leave us.

Within a minute they are quarrelling bitterly about
Emilia, Palamon, like an absurd schoolboy, declaring 'I
saw her first'. Another effective piece of irony is afforded
by their mutual envy: Palamon is envious of Arcite's
banishment, and Arcite envious of Palamon because he is
allowed to remain in prison near Emilia. The scene is
effective, but I should mention, perhaps, that when the
play was performed at the Old Vic between the wars,
the audience laughed at the quarrel; but this may have
been due to the acting, the actors showing that they were
conscious of the absurdities of some of the dialogue.

At the beginning of Act II Shakespeare's hand is once
more apparent in the opening soliloquy of Arcite:

> O Queene *Emilia*,
> Fresher than May, sweeter
> Than her gold buttons on the bowes, or all
> Th'enamelld knackes o' the Meade or garden! yea,
> We challenge too the bancke of any Nymph,
> That makes the streame seeme flowers; thou, O Iewell
> O' th wood, o' th world, hast likewise blest a place
> With thy sole presence!

Not only was Fletcher incapable of producing what
Murry called 'this unearthly melody of a shattered blank-
verse rhythm', and what Theodore Spencer beautifully

described as 'the caught breath, the broken wonder, the magical invocation . . . trembling through a shattered rhythm into words', but the lines are manifestly written by the author of similar passages in *Pericles*, *Cymbeline*, and *The Winter's Tale*. The jewel image is taken up in the last speech of the play when Theseus refers to Emilia as 'your stolen jewel'.

Shakespeare may have written a few more speeches in this scene, but nearly all critics are agreed that it soon drops into typical Fletcherian cadences and sentimentality:

> brave soules in shades,
> That have dyde manly, which will seeke of me
> Some newes from earth, they shall get none but this,
> That thou art brave and noble.

One of the difficulties confronting Shakespeare and Fletcher in dramatizing Chaucer's tale was to avoid monotony in the quarrels of the lovers. In the prison scene the warmest friendship is immediately followed by a bitter quarrel. In the May Day scene Arcite's pity for Palamon is immediately followed by Palamon's appearance, in shackles, and shaking his fist at Arcite. But the kinsmen are reconciled when Arcite promises to bring a sword and armour so that they can fight a duel. Two scenes later, when Arcite brings food, the two men are cordial for a few minutes, but the scene ends in another quarrel. Three scenes later, when Arcite brings sword and armour, they are again reconciled; and they respect each other more at the moment of their duel than ever before. Although there is an element of absurdity in all this, caused partly by the change of attitude to chivalric love during the two centuries which had elapsed since Chaucer's death, Fletcher is extraordinarily skilful in ringing the changes on this love–hate relationship. But in all these scenes, I think, it is fair to say, there is not a single memorable line. This is not because Fletcher, like Mr Eliot, was trying to write poetic drama which the audience would not recognize as verse.

The best of Fletcher's scenes is that which follows the interruption of the duel by Theseus. It follows roughly the same pattern as the first scene of the play. Theseus condemns both the kinsmen to death, and (as in the first scene) he is urged to change his mind first by the antiphonal pleading of Emilia and Hippolyta, and then by his friend Pirithous. Emilia first pleads for the substitution of banishment for death. Theseus refuses on the ground that they would then kill each other. Emilia claims that he had made a prior promise to her never to deny her anything, and asks that they should not only be banished, but should be made to swear never to make her their contention. Both Palamon and Arcite refuse to accept these conditions. Theseus then decides that one shall be killed and the other shall marry Emilia; but although Palamon and Arcite agree to this, Emilia refuses to choose between them. Theseus finally decides that Palamon and Arcite shall each engage in a tournament, each accompanied by three knights; the winner shall obtain Emilia as his bride, the loser, and his three friends, shall lose their heads. They all agree to this proposal. It is a scene which brings out Fletcher's best qualities. It does not require any depth of psychological understanding because the whole situation is theatrical rather than realistic; but the speeches are forcefully written, and the debate, within its convention, is exciting.

Effective too, in its preposterous way, is the scene in Act IV, in which Emilia compares the portraits of Palamon and Arcite and tries to choose between them. Her oscillation between her two suitors and her inability to choose between them is a means of preserving suspense, though by making her come to Palamon second Fletcher prepares the way for the ending. The audience are thus made to feel that everything comes right in the end, though they cannot be sure at this stage of the play what the ending will be.

Shakespeare seems to have contributed the whole of the fifth act except the second scene and the first eighteen lines of the first. The invocations of Mars, Venus, and Diana were the climax of Chaucer's tale, as they are of the play; and Shakespeare, without any verbal borrowing, takes the general argument of two of his speeches from Chaucer. Arcite's invocation of Mars is perhaps coloured by Elizabethan views on the social function of war. Dudley Digges, for example, Shakespeare's neighbour, had argued in *Four Paradoxes* that war is better than 'luxurious idleness', and that peace is apt to lead to dissension,

> when idleness ministers each active humour fit occasion of working, to the indangering of most healthful bodies, when quiet security gives busy heads leisure to divide the commonwealth into contentious factions.

In discussing the *Coriolanus* story he speaks of war in medical terms. Just as a poison like mercury can be used to purge and cleanse, so war can purge the diseases of the commonwealth. This idea was made easy to Shakespeare's contemporaries by the theory of correspondences between the body politic and the microcosm, as well as by the fact that physicians had frequent recourse to bleeding. So Arcite addresses Mars as

> thou grand decider
> Of dusty and old tytles, that healst with blood
> The earth when it is sicke, and cur'st the world
> O' the pluresie of people.

The surge and thunder of Shakespeare's final style is better illustrated by the beginning of the speech:

> Thou mighty one, that with thy power hast turnd
> Greene Neptune into purple; whose Approach
> Comets prewarne; whose havocke in vast Feild
> Vnearthed skulls proclaime; whose breath blowes downe
> The teeming Ceres foyzon; who dost plucke
> With hand armypotent from forth blew clowdes
> The masond Turrets; that both mak'st and break'st
> The stony girthes of cities; me thy puple,
> Yongest follower of thy Drom, instruct this day
> With military skill, that to thy lawde
> I may advance my streamer, and by thee
> Be stil'd the Lord o' th day.

Shakespeare's use of words was still as vigorous as ever, and so too was his habit of pictorializing his ideas. City walls are presented as 'stony girths'; and the idea that walls are built as a protection in war, and destroyed in the course of war, is condensed into the deliberately harsh phrase 'mak'st and break'st'. The destruction of castles or towers is presented in a hyperbolical picture of Mars plucking them from among the clouds. Some words – *unearthed*, *prewarn*, and *masoned* – Shakespeare had not used at all; and *armipotent* had previously been used in deliberately bombastic passages.

The speech is beautifully contrasted with the slow movement of Emilia's address to Diana, with its long roll of epithets and cold imagery:

> O sacred, shadowie, cold, and constant Queene,
> Abandoner of Revells, mute, contemplative,
> Sweet, solitary, white, as chaste and pure
> As winde fand snow.

It is noteworthy that the impression of purity is maintained by the use not only of such epithets and images as the ones I have just quoted, but also by using 'maculate' for stained, reminding us of its opposite, immaculate. There is the same continuing experimentation with vocabulary – Shakespeare had not before used abandoner, unsentenced, or pretender, nor the hyphenated wind-fanned, bride-habited, and maiden-hearted. There is the same felicity of phrasing as in the words 'thy rare green eye' and the description of Diana as 'our Generall of Ebbs and Flowes'.

Palamon's speech, addressed to Venus, is as masterly as the other two; but as Theodore Spencer alone has noticed, it is very strange. It is quite unlike the corresponding speech in *The Knight's Tale*, and at first sight it seems to be inappropriate both to the romantic love-rivalry of the play and to the character of Palamon. It begins with conventional praise of Venus, but quickly develops into a satirical account of her power, becoming more and more grotesque as it progresses. Venus makes 'A Criple florish with his Crutch'; she makes the bachelor of seventy sing lays of love; she makes a gouty man of eighty, with one foot in the grave, marry and beget an heir, his wife swearing it was his, and who, asks Palamon, would not believe her? Venus is finally addressed

> O thou that from eleven to ninetie raign'st
> In mortall bosomes.

Although Palamon speaks of her as 'most soft sweet goddess', the picture we have of her is of an imperious and cruel creature who holds gods and mortals at her mercy. Palamon himself who bears her yoke 'As 'twere a wreath of Roses', finds it 'heavier than Lead it selfe, stings more than Nettles'. In the rest of the speech Palamon boasts that he has 'never been foul-mouthed' against Venus's law, that he has never betrayed a woman or committed adultery, that he has objected to bawdy conversation, and that he avoids licentious company. The pleasanter side of love is not represented.

It is obviously absurd to suppose that Shakespeare, who not long before had written love-scenes for Perdita and Florizel and for Ferdinand and Miranda, was putting his own personal sentiments into Palamon's mouth. There would seem to be three good dramatic reasons for this satirical speech. In the first place, Palamon is rightly concerned with Venus's power – the power 'Even with an ey-glance to choke Mars's Drom' – because his rival is appealing to the power of Mars. And the power of

Venus is most plainly displayed, not in the mutual attraction of the young and handsome, but in the conquest of the gods – Mars and Diana – and in the miraculous reversal of nature's laws, the healing of the sick and impotent, and in her power over the senile. Secondly, there are indications – in Fletcher's scenes as well as Shakespeare's – of Palamon's disillusioned temperament. It is apparent in the scene in which he first appears. Even in the prison scene he claims that he sees through the vain pleasures of this world; and Emilia, describing his portrait, speaks of him as

> swarth and meagre, of an eye as heavy
> As if he had lost his mother.

In a later scene she speaks of his 'menacing aspect', his 'frowns', his 'melancholy' and 'darker humours'. The third reason why Shakespeare wrote this kind of speech is that Palamon has indeed found Venus's yoke heavier than lead, more stinging than nettles. It has caused him to quarrel with his kinsman; and he is faced at this moment in the play with the tragic fight. If he wins, the man he has loved will be executed, a bitter price to pay for the winning of Emilia. If he loses, he and his three innocent companions will be executed. It is arguable, perhaps, that by intruding such realistic considerations, Shakespeare was in danger of shattering the conventions in which the play was written; but I would suggest that it has something of the same effect as the frequent touches of realism in the most romantic comedies.

Mars, Venus, and Diana all answer their votaries' prayers, but not in the way they expect. Arcite prays for victory – to be styled lord of the day – and he wins the fight and loses Emilia. Palamon asks for success in love, but he achieves Emilia not by winning the fight but by the accidental death of Arcite. Emilia prays that the one who loves her best should win her, and we are meant to suppose that Palamon, who had originally hailed her as a goddess, was a truer lover than Arcite, who immediately desired her. Arcite confesses he was false to Palamon, because Palamon was the first to see Emilia and proclaim his love. We are not meant, presumably, to take this too seriously.

The stage-directions in this scene are as elaborate as in the first scene of the play, and they show that there must have been a considerable element of spectacle. When Arcite and his followers fall on their faces before the altar of Mars

> there is heard clanging of Armor, with a short Thunder, as the burst of a Battaile, whereupon they all rise and bow to the Altar.

At the altar of Venus 'music is heard, and doves are seen to flutter'; and the entrance of Emilia is even more elaborate:

> Still Musicke of Records. Enter Emilia in white, her haire about her shoulders, wearing a wheaten wreath; one in white holding up her traine, her haire stuck with flowers; One before her carrying a silver Hynde, in which is conveyed Incense and sweet odours, which is set upon the Altar of Diana, her maides standing aloofe, she sets fire to it; then they curtsey and kneele.

These are probably Shakespeare's own directions, since the hind is the centre of one of his image-clusters.

# Shakespeare as Collaborator

Shakespeare is more successful here than he had been with the appearance of Jupiter in *Cymbeline*; and he may have avoided the descent of Mars, Venus, and Diana because he felt that the corresponding scenes in *Cymbeline* and *Pericles* had not quite come off in performance.

I mentioned earlier the continual reference by Shakespeare to the gods, an appropriate preparation for the last act in which the gods appear to intervene in human affairs. These references are resumed in the last scenes. Arcite resigns himself to the will of the gods when he tells Palamon:

> So hoyst we
> The sayles, that must these vessells port even where
> The heavenly Lymiter pleases.

Emilia, believing that Palamon is to be executed, demands:

> Oh all you heavenly powers, where is your mercy?

Palamon, seeing the dying Arcite, exclaims:

> O miserable end of our alliance!
> The gods are mightie.

Theseus urges him to thank the gods that he is still living, and claims that 'the deities have showed due justice'. In the last speech Shakespeare attempts to round off his references to fortune and the gods by showing that the gods work through the operations of fortune.

> Never Fortune
> Did play a subtler Game: the conquerd triumphes,
> The victor has the Losse; yet in the passage
> The gods have beene most equall.

Later on in the same speech Theseus declares that

> the gods my justice
> Take from my hand, and they themselves become
> The Executioners.

And at the end he addresses the gods as

> O you heavenly Charmers,
> What things you make of us! For what we lacke
> We laugh, for what we have are sorry; still
> Are children in some kind. Let us be thankefull
> For that which is, and with you leave dispute
> That are above our question.

These lines, unless Shakespeare wrote part of *Cardenio*, are probably his last dramatic poetry. They do not imply that all is for the best in the best of all possible worlds, but neither is there any of the boredom and bitterness which Strachey found in the later plays of Shakespeare. We are left with a sense of mystery, the impossibility for man to understand the workings of providence, and of gratitude for life. I am reminded of some of the last words of a great writer of our own day, D. H. Lawrence:

For man, the vast marvel is to be alive. For man, as for flower and beast and bird, the supreme triumph is to be most vividly, most perfectly alive. Whatever the unborn and the dead may know, they cannot know the beauty, the marvel of being alive in the flesh. The dead may look after the afterwards. But the magnificent here and now of life in the flesh is ours, and ours alone, and ours only for a time.

I think it is significant that nearly all Shakespeare's last plays contain theophanies. Diana appears in *Pericles*;

Jupiter appears in *Cymbeline*; in *The Winter's Tale* there is an oracle and a vision; in *Henry VIII* a vision. All these plays contain references to God or the gods in their final speeches, and the epilogue of *The Tempest* ends with a prayer for forgiveness:

> my ending is despair
> Unless I be reliev'd by prayer,
> Which pierces so that it assaults
> Mercy itself, and frees all faults.
> As you from crimes would pardon'd be,
> Let your indulgence set me free.

In this respect *The Two Noble Kinsmen* conforms to the pattern of the plays of the last period. In other respects it differs considerably. Shakespeare is no longer obsessed with the necessity of forgiveness; he no longer deals with the reconciling of the fathers through the love of the children, with the restoration of the lost wife or child, with the recovery of a lost kingdom. Instead of the evil jealousy of Leontes and Posthumus, the murderous ambition of Antonio and Sebastian, there is only the comparatively sympathetic rivalry of Palamon and Arcite – the evil Creon never appears.

The plot of the play does not really allow much depth or subtlety of characterization. If, for example, Emilia's dilemma were allowed to be more than pathetic, if she were given a will of her own or the reality of an Imogen, the ending of the play would be more difficult to accept. In any case Fletcher lacked the poetic sensitiveness to develop Emilia along the lines of her portrait in the third scene of the play. But it is quite possible that the play-

146

goers at the Blackfriars preferred the slickness, the smart-
ness, and the sentimentality of the Fletcher scenes to the
gnarled toughness of Shakespeare's final style.

It is reasonable to suppose that the play was written in
something of a hurry. Perhaps Shakespeare, on one of his
last visits to London, was prevailed upon to help his old
fellows by writing something for the Blackfriars theatre,
as they were short of new plays for the forthcoming
season. Shakespeare, who wished to return to Stratford
within a fortnight, agreed to sketch out a play and to
write as much as he could in the time. Fletcher, who may
have collaborated with him already in *Henry VIII*, would
write the remaining scenes, and make any necessary
alterations in the parts written by Shakespeare. It is not a
play that adds anything to his reputation; but no other
English dramatist, then or since then, has equalled the
dramatic verse in the first scenes of Act I and Act V.

# VIII

# *Cardenio*

A play entitled *Cardenio* was acted at Court by the King's Men in 1613; and this was ascribed by Humphrey Moseley, when he entered it in the Stationers' Register in 1653, to 'Mr Fletcher and Shakespeare'. The assumption was a reasonable one, since Shakespeare and Fletcher, as we have seen, had collaborated about the same time in *The Two Noble Kinsmen* and (many critics still believe) in *Henry VIII*. Apparently Moseley never published *Cardenio*; but in 1727 a play entitled *Double Falsehood*, prepared for the stage by Lewis Theobald and ascribed by him to Shakespeare alone, was performed with considerable success. This, like the lost play, was based on an episode in Shelton's translation of *Don Quixote* (Book I). *Double Falsehood* is based on the same story, though the names of the characters are different, and there are a few minor alterations in the plot. Henriquez,[1] after violating Violante,[2] falls in love with Julio's[3] betrothed, Leonora.[4] Her parents agree to the marriage, and Julio arrives in time for the ceremony. Leonora, who has intended to kill herself, swoons and takes sanctuary. Julio, mad with grief, overhears Violante, who disguised as a boy has just escaped the amorous attentions of a herdsman,

[1] Fernando.    [2] Dorotea.    [3] Cardenio.    [4] Luscinda.

blaming Henriquez. He makes himself known to her. By the intervention of Roderick, Henriquez's elder brother, Violante appeals to the Duke. Henriquez repents and marries Violante, and Julio marries Leonora.

*Double Falsehood* was published in 1728; and, in the dedicatory epistle, Theobald told George Dodington:

> I flatter Myself, that if You shall think fit to pronounce this Piece genuine, it will silence the Censures of those *Unbelievers*, who think it is impossible a Manuscript of *Shakespeare* could so long have lain dormant; and who are blindly paying Me a greater Compliment than either They design, or I can merit, while they cannot but confess Themselves *pleased*, yet would fain insinuate that they are *imposed upon*. I should esteem it some Sort of *Virtue*, were I able to commit *so agreeable a Cheat*.

In the Preface Theobald disclaimed the need of offering proof of Shakespeare's authorship:

> The Success, which this Play has met with from the Town in the Representation, (to say nothing of the Reception it found from those Great Judges, to whom I have had the Honour of communicating it in Manuscript;) has almost made the Purpose of a Preface unnecessary: . . . It has been alledg'd as incredible, that such a Curiosity should be stifled and lost to the World for above a Century. To this my Answer is short; that tho' it never till now made its Appearance on the Stage, yet one of the Manuscript Copies, which I have, is of above Sixty Years Standing, in the Handwriting of Mr *Downes*, the famous Old Prompter; and, as I am credibly inform'd, was early in the Possession of the celebrated Mr *Betterton*, and by Him design'd to have been usher'd into the World. What Accident prevented This

Purpose of his, I do not pretend to know: or thro' what hands it had successively pass'd before that Period of Time. There is a Tradition (which I have from the Noble Person, who supply'd me with One of my Copies) that it was given by our Author, as a Present of Value, to a Natural Daughter of his, for whose sake he wrote it, in the Time of his Retirement from the Stage. Two Other Copies I have, (one of which I was glad to purchase at a very good Rate,) which may not, perhaps, be quite so Old as the Former; but One of Them is much more perfect, and had fewer Flaws and Interruptions in the Sense . . .

Others again, to depreciate the Affair, as they thought, have been pleased to urge, that tho' the Play may have some Resemblances of *Shakespeare*, yet the *Colouring, Diction*, and *Characters*, come nearer to the Style and Manner of FLETCHER. This, I think, is far from deserving of any Answer; I submit it to the Determination of better Judgments; tho' my Partiality for *Shakespeare* makes me wish, that Every Thing which is good, or pleasing, in our Tongue, had been owing to his Pen.

It is, perhaps, significant, that Theobald, in his second edition, substituted for the words 'in our Tongue' the words 'in that other great poet', as though he were less certain than he had been that the play was not by Fletcher.[1]

Theobald's account is not above suspicion. He is vague on matters where one would like him to be precise. He does not tell us how he obtained possession of the Downes manuscript, nor the name of the 'Noble Person'

[1] The point is made by R. F. Jones, *Lewis Theobald* (N.Y., 1919), p. 103.

who supplied him with one of the manuscripts, nor does he make it clear whether there were three or four manuscripts in all,[1] nor does he give us the names of the 'Great Judges' to whom he showed one manuscript. The tradition of Shakespeare's natural daughter reads like an invention, since the poet's plays were not his own property. It is odd that all the manuscripts should have disappeared, and, unless we assume that Theobald changed his mind about the authorship, it is strange that he did not include the play in his edition of Shakespeare. It is a calamity, if he really possessed an authentic Shakespearian manuscript, that he should have published only a version which was avowedly altered, and which was probably as much a perversion as his revisions of other Elizabethan plays.[2]

[1] Is the Downes copy the same as the one Theobald obtained from the 'Noble Person'?

[2] Theobald claimed that he had written the passage:

> Strike up, my Masters;
> But touch the Strings with a religious Softness:
> Teach sound to languish on thro' Night's dull Ear,
> Till Melancholy start from her lazy Couch,
> And Carelessness grow Convert to Attention.

There are some passages as good as this in Theobald's adaptation of *Richard II*. In this version he eliminates the first two acts of Shakespeare's play, though he salvages some of the more famous lines and gives them to other characters. He adds a love interest – Aumerle loves Lady Piercy and is executed for conspiracy against Bolingbroke. The speech at the end of Act I gives a favourable idea of Theobald's talents as a poet:

> Thou chid'st me well,
> For setting up my Rest in giddy State,
> And Ostentation of despised Empire.
> By Heav'n, I want no Kingdom having thee:
> Let restless spirits parcel out the Globe,

But, when all allowances have been made, it is remarkable, to say the least, that, if the play was Theobald's own, he should have chosen for his plot one which the author of *Cardenio* used, for there is no reason to believe that he knew of the Court performance – he denied that the play had ever been acted – and if he had known of Moseley's entry he would have used it to support the play's authenticity, rather than have denied that Fletcher had had a hand in it. There may, perhaps, have been a tradition that such a play existed, but there seems to be no record of such a tradition. On the whole, it seems more likely that Theobald possessed at least one manuscript than that he himself was the sole author of the play.

It has been generally recognized that some scenes of the play, including especially those of the last two acts, appear to be in Fletcher's manner, and that these seem to be less adulterated with Theobald's pastiche than other parts of the play.[1] Of course Fletcher is more easily imitated than Shakespeare; but Violante's plaint in Act IV, Scene II,

> And sweat for Limit and Prerogative;
> Vexing the States, in which they Monarchize,
> With Starts and Tumults of ungovern'd Pride.
> I here disclaim all Thrones; nor will embroil
> A Nation's Safety in my doubtful Quarrel.
> All you, that wou'd be safe, fly from my Side:
> Crowns shall no more from Love my Thoughts divide.

But *Richard II* contains no passages added by Theobald as good as the best in *Double Falsehood*, and none which strike the reader as effectively Shakespearian.

[1] Walter Graham in his edition of *Double Falsehood* (Cleveland, 1920) gives various metrical tests, on which the following table is based. (I should mention, however, that I cannot find more than a

for example, recalls, without actually echoing, the laments
of Aspatia in *The Maid's Tragedy*:

> I cannot get this false Man's Memory
> Out of my Mind. You Maidens, that shall live
> To hear my mournful Tale, when I am Ashes,
> Be wise; and to an Oath no more give Credit,
> To Tears, to Vows, (false Both!) or any Thing
> A Man shall promise, than to Clouds, that now
> Bear such a pleasing Shape, and now are nothing.
> For they will cozen, (if They may be cozen'd,)
> The very Gods they worship – Valour, Justice,
> Discretion, Honesty, and all they covet,
> To make them seeming Saints, are but the Wiles
> By which these *Syrens* lure us to Destruction.
> (IV. ii. 60 ff.)

Even here one may doubt whether Fletcher would have
compared men to sirens.

---

few of the nineteen weak-endings and light-endings in the 'Shakespearian' scenes listed by Graham.)

|  | *Double Falsehood* | | *Two Noble Kinsmen* | | *Henry VIII* | |
|---|---|---|---|---|---|---|
|  | W.S. | J.F. | W.S. | J.F. | W.S. | J.F. |
| Feminine endings percentage | 32 | 44 | 21 | 62 | 28 | 58 |
| Run on lines percentage | 21 | 15 | 52 | 26 | 55 | 26 |
| Weak and light percentage | 2·7 | ·39 | 8·1 | ·23 | 10·8 | ·22 |

It will be observed that in each play there are more feminine endings
in the scenes ascribed to Fletcher, and fewer run-on lines and weak
and light endings. Not much weight should be placed on these
figures, since Theobald's own alterations would upset the percentages – particularly in the non-Fletcherian scenes – and we cannot
be certain that his style in this play was the same as his style in the
additions to *Richard II*. He might have been influenced by the
difference between Shakespeare's later style and that of 1595.

# Shakespeare as Collaborator

The remaining scenes of the play – those apparently not Fletcher's – are the only ones which might have a Shakespearian foundation. Theobald might be expected to do more revision of scenes written in the convoluted style of the Shakespearian part of *The Two Noble Kinsmen* than of the more straightforward style of Fletcher's plays, so that it would be vain to expect any certain traces of Shakespeare. An eighteenth-century reviser might be expected to make short work of weak and light-endings,[1] so that their absence need not rule out the possibility of a Shakespearian original. What is more suspicious is the presence of wholesale echoes of Shakespeare's previous work. There are, of course, many echoes, particularly in *Cymbeline*, but these are of a different kind. Some scenes in *Double Falsehood* look as though they were manufactured by Theobald, with a copy of Shakespeare's works open in front of him.[2] In the first scene, for example, apart from possible echoes of *1 Henry IV*, there is what appears to be a certain echo of Polonius's words about Laertes:[3]

> why he hath of late
> By Importunity, the strain'd Petition,
> Wrested our Leave of Absence from the Court.
> (I. i. 26–8)

[1] But see previous note.
[2] Cf. L. Schwartzstein, *N.Q.* (1954), pp. 471–2.
[3] Cf. *Hamlet*, I. ii. 58–60.

> He hath, my lord, wrung from me my slow leave
> By laboursome petition, and at last
> Upon his will I seal'd my hard consent.

Ophelia in the next scene says that she has 'of late' received tenders of affection from Hamlet, and that he has 'importuned' her.

A prose passage in the second scene contains two echoes from *Hamlet* – of Laertes' departure and of the Prince's promise to go to his mother's closet 'by and by':[1]

> I must bethink me of some Necessaries, without which you might be unfurnish'd: And my Supplies shall at all Convenience follow You. Come to my Closet by and by; I would there speak with You. (I. ii. 54–7)

In the second scene, too, we are reminded of Polonius's advice to Ophelia:[2]

> I speak not This altogether to unbend your Affections to him: But the meaning of what I say is, that you set such Price upon yourself to him, as Many, and much His betters, would buy you at; (and reckon those Virtues in you at the rate of their Scarcity;) to which if he come not up, you remain for a better Mart. (I. ii. 204 ff.)

In the same scene, where Leonora and Julio part, the obvious model is *Troilus and Cressida*:[3]

> *Leon.* But when go you?
> *Jul.* To-morrow, Love; so runs the Duke's Command;
>    Stinting our Farewell-kisses, cutting off
>    The Forms of Parting, and the Interchange
>    Of thousand precious Vows, with Haste too rude.
>       (I. ii. 138–42)

Compare Troilus's words:

>    And suddenly: where injury of chance
>    *Puts back leave-taking, justles roughly by*

[1] Cf. *Hamlet*, I. iii. 1, III. ii. 353, 411.
[2] Cf. *Hamlet*, I. iii. 90–135.
[3] Cf. *Troilus and Cressida*, IV. iv. 35–50. At least the passage is closer to Shakespeare's lines, quoted below, than to the corresponding passage in Dryden's version.

*All time of pause; rudely beguiles our lips*
*Of all rejoindure; forcibly prevents*
*Our lock'd embrasures; strangles our dear vows*
Even in the birth of our own labouring breath.
We two that with so many *thousand* sighs
Did buy each other, must poorly sell ourselves
With the *rude* brevity and discharge of one.
Injurious Time now with a robber's haste
Crams his rich thievery up, he knows not how.
As many *farewells* as be stars in heaven,
With distinct breath and consign'd kisses to them
He fumbles up into a loose adieu,
And *scants* us with a single famish'd *kiss*
Distasted with the salt of broken tears.

A few lines later there is another echo of the same scene of *Troilus and Cressida*, and also of the earlier scene where the lovers plight their troth: [1]

O let Assurance, strong as Words can bind,
Tell thy pleas'd Soul, I will be wond'rous faithful;
True, as the Sun is to his Race of Light,
As Shade to Darkness, as Desire to Beauty:
And when I swerve, let Wretchedness o'ertake me,
Great as e'er Falshood met, or change can merit.
(I. ii. 153 ff.)

Although there can be little doubt that such passages were written by Theobald – or, less probably, that he was rewriting an earlier imitation of Shakespeare – there are other passages and phrases which would appear to be beyond his powers. In the first scene, for example, the use

[1] Cf. *Troilus and Cressida*, III. ii. 165–203, and especially 'As sun to day' (185) and 'If I be false or swerve a hair from truth . . . Upbraid my falsehood' (191, 198).

of *heirs* as a verb – 'heirs my better Glories' – and the line –

> But I, my Fears weighing his unweigh'd Course –

may be singled out. In the second scene, likewise, there are at least two passages which strike the reader as genuinely Elizabethan, though definitely not Fletcherian:

> I do not see that Fervour in the Maid,
> Which Youth and Love should kindle. She consents,
> As 'twere to feed without an Appetite;
> Tells me, she is content; and plays the coy one,
> Like Those that subtly make their Words their Ward,
> Keeping Address at Distance. This Affection
> Is such a feign'd One, as will break untouch'd;
> Dye frosty, e'er it can be thaw'd; while mine,
> Like to a Clime beneath *Hyperion's* Eye,
> Burns with one constant Heat.
> (I. ii. 58 ff.)

The imagery of this passage, the playing on *Words* and *Ward*, and the rhythm are either Shakespearian or a remarkably clever imitation. Almost as effective is this exchange between Julio and Leonora:

> *Jul.*   Urge not suspicions of what cannot be;
>   You deal unkindly, mis-becomingly,
>   I'm loth to say: For All that waits on you,
>   Is graced, and graces. – No Impediment
>   Shall bar my Wishes, but such grave Delays
>   As Reason presses Patience with; which blunt not,
>   But rather whet our Loves. Be patient, Sweet.

157

*Leon.* Patient! What else? My Flames are in the Flint.
　　　Haply, to lose a Husband I may weep;
　　　Never, to get One: When I cry for Bondage,
　　　Let Freedom quit me.
　　　　　　　　　(I. ii. 101)

The third scene contains an apparent echo from *Romeo and Juliet* – [1]

　　A Gleam of Day breaks sudden from her Window –
　　　　　　　　　(I. iii. 26)

but it also contains one striking hyperbole:

　　　The Court, whereof Report,
　　And Guess alone inform her, she will rave at,
　　As if she there sev'n Reigns had slander'd Time.
　　　　　　　　　(I. iii. 16–8)

The following lines contain a word, *absonant*, never used by Shakespeare, but the kind of word which he did use in his last period, together with a typical Shakespearian contrast between an artificial perfume and the scent of the violet:

　　　Home, my Lord,
　　What you can say is most unseasonable; what sing,
　　Most absonant and harsh: Nay, your Perfume,
　　Which I smell hither, cheers not my Sense
　　Like our Field-violet's Breath.
　　　　　　　　　(I. iii. 52–6)

(Possibly a word – *now* [?] – has dropped out of the fourth of these lines.)

[1] *Romeo and Juliet*, II. ii. 2–3:
　　But, soft! what light through yonder window breaks?
　　It is the east, and Juliet is the sun!

In later scenes there are some good lines, but nothing beyond the powers of a good imitator, e.g.:

> I am now become
> The Tomb of my own Honour: a dark Mansion,
> For Death alone to dwell in.          (II. ii. 30)

> Now Summer Bliss and gawdy Days are gone,
> My Lease in 'em's expir'd.          (III. ii. 34)

There is no iterative imagery in the play, and no image-clusters. But there is no iterative imagery in *The Two Noble Kinsmen*; and it may be mentioned that Dryden cut some of the cooking imagery from *Troilus and Cressida*. Iterative imagery, if there were any, could not be expected to survive Theobald's revision.

It is clearly impossible to come to any definite conclusions about *Double Falsehood*, but it seems more likely that Theobald was working on an old manuscript than that he knew of Moseley's entry of *Cardenio* and that he composed scenes in two different styles while asserting Shakespeare's sole authorship. He probably believed at first that the play was by Shakespeare, but was afterwards sufficiently shaken in his view not to include the play in his edition of Shakespeare. If, indeed, he had one or more manuscripts, there would be strong reason to believe that *Double Falsehood* was a debased version of *Cardenio*, and equally strong reasons for believing that the original authors were Shakespeare and Fletcher. With few exceptions, critics have endeavoured to escape from this conclusion. Those who think that Theobald was not wholly responsible for the play have argued for some other Jacobean dramatist – Daborne, Davenport, Rowley, Shirley, and Beaumont. There is no need to argue the case against any of these dramatists, since there is no evidence, either internal or external, that any of them had a hand in *Cardenio*. But one can understand the desire to relieve Shakespeare of all responsibility for a play which, at least in its present form, can add nothing to his reputation.

THE END

# INDEX

# Index